Caribbean Cookery

Floella Benjamin was born in Trinidad and is one of
six children. The family moved to England where
Floella completed her education. After leaving school
she spent a short time in the world of banking but
soon found her way into show business.

She appeared in several successful West End shows
including *Jesus Christ Superstar*, *The Black Mikado* and
The Husband in Law. She has appeared in numerous
drama and comedy shows on television such as *The
Gentle Touch*, *Angels*, *Crown Court*, *Maybury*, *Mixed
blessings*, *Within These Walls*, *Waterloo Sunset*, *Hole in
Babylon*, *Bergerac* and *Strangers*. She has also guested
on many game and panel shows and was critically
acclaimed for her film portrayal of Miriam in the
British film *Black joy*.

Floella is probably best known by children
throughout the country as presenter of BBC's
PlaySchool and *PlayAway*.

Floella has also written several best selling children's
books, and activity books for youngsters called
Floella's Fun Book (Methuen), *Why the Agouti has no
Tail* (Hutchinson's Childrens Books), *Fall about with
Flo* (Beaver) and *Floella's Funniest Jokes*.

She is also very active in a variety of charities
including Save the Children, Birthright and Oxfam.

Caribbean Cookery

Floella Benjamin
Illustrated by Jennifer Northway

Rider

London Melbourne Auckland Johannesburg

First published in 1986 by Century Hutchinson Ltd,
Brookmount House, 62–65 Chandos Place, Convent
Garden, London WC2N 4NW

Century Hutchinson Publishing Group (Australia) Pty Ltd,
16–22 Church Street, Hawthorn, Melbourne, Victoria 3122

Century Hutchinson Group (NZ) Ltd,
32–34 View Road, PO Box 40–086, Glenfield, Auckland 10

Century Hutchinson Group (SA) Pty Ltd,
PO Box 337, Bergvlei 2012, South Africa

Set in Linotron Bembo by Wyvern Typsetting Ltd, Bristol
Printed and bound in Great Britain by The Guernsey Press
Co. Ltd, Guernsey, C.I.

British Library Cataloguing in Publication Data
Benjamin, Floella
    Caribbean cookery.
    1. Cookery, Caribbean
    I. Title
    641.59'1821   TX716.A1
    ISBN 0–7126–9474–9

To Mammy and Daddy

Contents

Acknowledgements

First of all, a very special thanks must go to my parents to whom this book is dedicated – my mother, who undoubtedly cooks the tastiest food in the world, and my dad, whose own favourite recipes and vast knowledge of Caribbean's history, culture and traditions helped make this book possible.

I must also thank a great many people – my husband, friends, relatives and total strangers – whose enthusiasm in helping me to compile the recipes for the book was overwhelming.

In my search for information about the Caribbean I was helped immensely by the Reference Library at the Commonwealth Institute. Their assistance was much appreciated.

A word of thanks also to the friendly stallholders of Brixton market, in particular Tina's Tropical Foods in the Granville Arcade, who allowed me to use their stall for the cover photograph of this book.

Finally, thanks once again to the many people who, when asked about their favourite recipes and recollections of the Caribbean, took such time and effort to write them down on scraps of paper and, with a faraway look in ther eyes, shared their childhood memories with me. I hope this book makes them proud!

Introduction

The Caribbean Islands stretch in a 1700-mile arc from the coast of South America to Florida.

Most people refer to these enormously varied islands as the West Indies. Of course, the West Indies form only a small part of the Caribbean chain and to group all the islands under one heading is simplifying things to say the least!

From Cuba to Trinidad history has formed an extraordinary mixture of cultures, giving each island a wealth of customs and, of course, culinary styles.

The original inhabitants of the islands were the Arawak Indians, also known as Tainos. They were a gentle race which lived by fishing and cultivating cassava, sweet potato, pawpaw, corn, guava, mammy apples, garlic and tobacco. These peaceful Arawaks were no match for the warlike and cannibalistic Caribs, who came in canoes from Paraguay. The Caribs swept across the islands raiding the Arawaks, and when the Spanish arrived in the fifteenth century in search of gold they found Caribs well established on many of the islands. It took the Spanish, French, British and Dutch almost three hundred years to virtually exterminate the tribe. Even so there are still a few pure Caribs today living in a village on the island of Dominica. They still practise some of the traditions of their thirteenth-century ancestors and the memory of the Carib people still lives on in the very name 'Caribbean'.

Caribbean cuisine has been influenced by the European countries that colonized the islands and because of this the style of cooking varies greatly from island to island. The French, Spanish, Dutch, Portuguese and British all played their part and when other nationalities, such as the East Indians, Indonesians and Chinese, arrived their styles of cooking were also absorbed. I was born in Trinidad so my style of cooking has a Trinidadian flavour. Trinidad's food has been influenced by the Spanish, Portuguese, French, Jews, Syrians, Chinese, Indians, British and Africans as well as the Carib Indians so you can imagine what an amazing range of techniques and flavours there are! The original inhabitants of the islands, the Arawaks, have also left their mark on the rules and traditions linked with the preparation and serving of dishes such as Jerked Pork and Pepper-pot Stew. It was from the Arawaks that the Spanish learnt how to smoke meat over an open fire. In fact the word 'barbecue' is an Arawak word.

Of course, the major change that took place in the Caribbean was the importation of the slaves from the continent of Africa. These people were forced to work the plantations of new, also imported, crops such as sugar cane and bananas.

The Caribbean became a thriving business territory for its European masters. Even the slaves themselves were traded in exchange for rum and sugar, and this too became a booming business.

It was these slaves, my ancestors, that are the basis of the Caribbean people today. The Ashanti, the Mocoes, the Ibos, the Mandingoes, the Senegalese, the Congolese and the Angolans brought with them their customs, religions and methods of cooking. Dukanoo and Fungi are two dishes that can be traced back to their African origins.

The enslaved African people were not allowed to eat fresh meat and instead were given rations of salted meat and fish and these are still very much part of Caribbean cuisine today. They did, however, manage to find alternatives to salt-fish and salt meat, the small animals that inhabit the islands, such as the agouti, the armadillo (tatou), the manicou (opposum) and iguana lizard, were and still are hunted and eaten. The slaves were given plots of land on which to grow their own crops and it was on these plots that they grew corn, okra, yam, ackee, callaloo and cocoa, which are also still part of our everyday diet.

The Caribbean islands have many religious festivals, the most famous being the pre-Lent carnivals which are celebrated for the three days leading up to Ash Wednesday. These carnivals were introduced to the islands by the French over two hundred years ago and now attract visitors from all over the world. It's a time for dressing up in fabulous costumes and 'jumping up' to steel band music. The most famous of these carnivals is held in Trinidad.

A traditional dish eaten at this time is Pigeon Peas and Rice. There is no religious reason for this, it's just because the pigeon peas are in season and can be eaten fresh. During the period of Lent only fish is eaten on Fridays.

Other festivals are held throughout the islands during July and August to celebrate the end of slavery. In Barbados the sugar cane cutters hold a harvest festival called 'Kadooment'. At Christmas and New Year in Jamaica and the Bahamas a grand festival called 'Junkanoo' is celebrated. It goes back to the days when the slaves were only allowed three days holiday a year and to celebrate they dressed up in symbolic costumes and danced through the streets. In fact the festival got its name from a slave called John Canoe, who was asked to organize a Christmas entertainment for the plantation owners. Over the years the name has changed, so has the reason for the celebration. Food and drink are an important part of all these celebrations. Christmas in particular is celebrated in style all over the Caribbean and traditional things like turkey and Christmas cake are eaten.

The Caribbean is a mixture of people of many religions and cultures all of whom have their own rituals and traditions relating to food, and it would be impossible to single out any particular customs that are common to all the islands.

It's worth noting that many islands have different names for the same fruit, vegetable, fish and, in some cases, dish. For example on some islands avocado pear is called 'zaboca' and aubergines are 'melongene' or 'garden eggs'. King fish is known as 'tassard' and salmon is 'weak fish' or 'bangomaree'. In Jamaica salt fish fritters are called 'Stamp and Go', while on Martinique they are known as 'Accra'! On Montserrat goat stew is 'Goat Water', whereas on Aruba and Curaçao it's called 'Stoba'! I have tried to give as many of these alternative names as possible and I hope you are not too confused.

Until the advent of cheap air travel the Caribbean was a place that few people had a chance to visit and those that did were catered for by large hotels where European and American dishes such as steak and chips and hamburgers were served; the local dishes were strictly for the locals. Thankfully things have changed and tourists are at last getting the chance to sample the delights of Caribbean food, now served with pride in the restaurants and hotels.

In the fifties and sixties many West Indians came to England. My family was amongst them and one of the difficulties we encountered was obtaining the ingredients for our traditional dishes. Plantain, sweet potato, okra and green bananas were almost impossible to find in shops and markets. Happily, that is no longer the case, due mainly to West Indians themselves organizing the importation of Caribbean produce. Now markets and shops throughout Britain sell most of the ingredients necessary to prepare traditional Caribbean dishes.

It has taken a long time for Caribbean cookery to become accepted in the world of international cuisine because of its complexities and variations, but it seems now that at last Caribbean food is growing in popularity, and quite rightly so. Presumably many people acquire a taste for the exciting flavours of the Caribbean while on holiday there. It is also encouraging to observe the appearance of Caribbean restaurants in many parts of Britain and the inclusion of Caribbean dishes on canteen menus. Some of the cookery programmes on television are also beginning to catch on and are featuring Caribbean dishes.

It is with this growing interest in Caribbean food as well as my own obvious interest in the subject that I have written this book. Over the years I have collected many traditional Caribbean recipes from friends and family, many of which have been passed on from generation to generation.

Although many of the ingredients used in the recipes are now easily available I've included some substitute ingredients in case people feel more at home with familiar foods or have difficulty obtaining some things. For example, red snapper can be replaced by trout or goat by lamb and so on. The flavour of the Caribbean can still be kept by using the spices and the cooking method in the recipe.

Vegetarians will find many exciting and interesting dishes both throughout this book and in the special vegetarian section which I have included with them in mind. Recipes such as Sweet Potato and Banana Casserole, Cheesy Yam and Fried Bhaji are well worth a try.

The people of the Caribbean have been using traditional homeopathic and herbal medicines for generations and many of the cures and remedies are still used in preference to modern drugs and I've included a short section on this subject.

I hope you enjoy cooking the recipes in this book and that they will introduce you to a whole new and exciting range of flavours and ingredients, many of which can easily share the plate with traditional English food. Try cooking some breadfruit in place of ordinary potatoes!

If you are planning a Caribbean meal I've included some suggested menus that might help and there is also a section on the specialities of the different islands.

Anyway, have fun, enjoy yourselves and remember 'cooking comes from the soul', so try experimenting and adding your own touches to the recipes.

Floella

Weights & Measures

The amounts given in my recipes are sufficient for four to six people unless I've said otherwise, and in the case of biscuits and cookies the amount made from the mixture depends on how large you make each biscuit. As I have already said, Caribbean cookery comes from the soul and therefore it is not an exact science. The weights and measures I have given are really only a guide and individual cooks vary the amounts according to their taste. My mum taught me to test the flavour as I am preparing a dish and adjust it accordingly, I hope you will do the same. But if you don't feel like experimenting to begin with, here is a conversion table.

Don't worry too much about being accurate. Feel free to round off small amounts.

Ounces/fluid ounces	Grammes/ml	Round off to
1	28	25
2	57	55
3	85	85
4	113	110
5 ($\frac{1}{4}$ pint)	142	145
6	170	175
7	198	200
8	226	225
9	255	250
10 ($\frac{1}{2}$ pint)	283	280
11	311	300
12	340	350
13	368	375
14	396	400
15 ($\frac{3}{4}$ pint)	428	425
16 (1 lb)	456	450
17	486	480
18	486	500
19	541	550
20 (1 pint)	569	570

Oven Temperatures

In the recipes I use the terms hot, medium and low for oven temperatures and what I consider to be the equivalent in Fahrenheit and Celsius. Of course, you know your own oven best so please use your own judgement and only use my equivalents as a guide. However, here is a standard conversion table showing oven temperatures in Celsius, Fahrenheit and the equivalent gas mark. Most of the recipes are not suitable for microwave ovens, but for the ones that are I have given approximate timings.

	°F	°C	Gas mark
Low	275	140	1
Medium	325	160	3
Medium hot	375	190	5
Hot	425	220	7
Very hot	475	240	9

Fruit

The Caribbean has always been associated with exotic fruit: just the mention of mango, guava or pawpaw conjures up exciting images. For me many of the fruits mentioned here bring back wonderful childhood memories. The mango season in Trinidad was a very exciting time and I remember as a child getting up at dawn and running to the mango trees in our garden to collect the fruits that had fallen during the night. In the guava season it took ages to reach school because of the stops we made at the laden guava bushes on the way. We even ate them green, which gave us terrible tummy ache.

It seemed to take for ever for the pawpaws to ripen, the waiting was excruciating. Oh . . . and the smell of freshly cut sugar cane was heavenly!

Tropical fruits are now more popular than ever and can be found in most high streets. They can be eaten fresh or used to make exotic desserts, ice creams, sorbets, drinks and even jams and pickles.

Nutritional Value

Caribbean fruit is very high in vitamins and minerals. Some are unusually high in nutritional value, such as mango and golden apple. Over the page is a list of fruits common to the Caribbean along with their nutritional values.

Ackee

This exotic fruit is only grown in Jamaica as far as I know. It is dark red in colour and when the fruit is ripe it splits open to reveal black seeds surrounded by white creamy flesh. Up to this point, ackee is poisonous, only the creamy part should be eaten and the seeds, skin and pink membrane, which is also poisonous, should be thrown away. I find it easier and safer to buy ackee in tins.

Although it is a fruit, ackee is cooked and served as a starter. One of the best-known dishes is Ackee and Salt Fish, a Jamaican speciality.

Fruit Per 100 g (4 oz)	Calories	Fat (g)	Protein (g)	Vit. C (mg)	Vit. A (mcg)	Calcium (mg)	Iron (mg)	Carbo-hydrate (g)
Ackee	30	0.2	0.9	78	—	37	1.7	7.3
Avocado	94	8.3	1.3	16	15	6	0.8	5.7
Banana	97	0.1	1.2	14	30	10	0.4	25.5
Cashew fruit	46	0.2	0.8	219	120	4	1.0	11.6
Coconut	296	27.2	3.5	4	—	13	1.8	13.7
Coconut milk	18	0.1	0.2	2	—	20	0.4	4.1
Golden apple or Pomsitea	95	—	1.0	40	50	20	1.2	23.0
Grandilla	20	0.2	0.7	15	—	14	0.8	4.3
Grapefruit	38	0.2	0.6	43	10	18	0.5	9.6
Guava	69	0.4	0.9	218	20	22	0.7	17.3
Lime	32	1.4	0.5	40	5	24	0.4	7.0
Mammy apple	47	0.2	0.6	16	90	13	0.4	12.1
Mango	59	0.2	0.5	53	630	12	0.8	15.5
Orange	42	0.2	0.8	42	20	34	0.6	10.5
Pawpaw (ripe)	32	0.1	0.5	46	110	20	0.4	8.3
Pineapple	52	0.2	0.4	61	15	18	0.5	13.7
Pomerac	51	0.4	0.8	14	653	90	0.2	12.5
Sapodilla	94	1.1	0.5	15	10	24	1.0	23.0
Shaddock	34	0.2	0.6	35	—	26	0.5	8.5
Sorrel	55	1.0	1.7	6	10	110	2.2	12.0
Soursop	60	0.4	1.0	26	5	24	0.5	14.9
Tamarind	272	0.4	3.1	6	20	54	1.0	71.8
Ugli fruit	40	0.2	0.8	55	20	25	0.6	10.5

To cook, remove and discard seeds, skin and pink membrane, soak flesh in salted water for about 10 minutes then drain and fry in oil. If using tinned ackee there's no need to soak.

Ackee Fritters

1 tin ackee
batter
oil to fry

Prepare a batter of flour, egg, salt and milk. Drain the ackee, dip into batter and fry in oil until golden. Serve on a bed of lettuce.

Avocado Pear

Known in Trinidad as zaboca and in other parts of the Caribbean as alligator pear, midshipman's butter or guacate.

It's a pear-shaped green- or purple-skinned fruit with a large stone inside. Avocado has a unique, delicate, nutty flavour and is perfect as a starter halved with an oil and vinegar dressing or sliced as part of a salad.

Zaboca and Pineapple Salad

1 pineapple
2 avocados
1 lettuce

125 ml (4 fl oz) mayonnaise
juice of 1 lime
black pepper

Peel and slice the avocados and pineapple. Arrange on a bed of lettuce keeping a quarter of the avocado aside for dressing.

Blend the mayonnaise, lime juice and the remaining avocado together and use as dressing for the salad.

Bananas

Not much can be said about bananas except that there are over twenty-five varieties, all of which are highly nutritious and delicious. The banana was brought by the Spanish from the Canaries in the sixteenth century and is today one of the main exports of many Caribbean islands.

The best time to eat bananas is when they are very ripe and brown spots are starting to cover the skin.

Frost and Flame Bananas

2 egg whites
50 g (2 oz) castor sugar
4 bananas

575 ml (1 pt) ice-cream (my
favourite is passion fruit or
tutti fruiti for this recipe)
50 ml (2 fl oz) rum

Beat egg whites, adding sugar slowly, until very stiff.

Peel bananas and slice lengthways. Cut each slice into three and arrange half the pieces in an oblong shape in an ovenproof dish. Place the block of ice-cream on top and cover with the rest of the banana pieces. Completely cover with the egg white mixture and place in a very hot pre-heated oven, 425°F (220°C, gas mark 7), for 5 minutes.

Warm the rum while the mixture is baking, pour over the baked bananas and set alight at the table.

Cashew Fruit

Cashew nuts are world famous but the fruit is not quite so well known outside the Caribbean. Cashew fruit is a red or yellow fleshy flower stalk 2–3 inches (5–7cm) in length at the end of which grows the nut.

The fruit makes a refreshing drink and also excellent jam.

Cashew Jam

175 g (6 oz) cashew fruit

175 g (6 oz) sugar

Wash and peel fruit and cut into small pieces.

Place in a heavy saucepan with the sugar and cook slowly until soft.

Allow to cool, pour into a jar and seal.

cashew apple and nut

Coconut

I feel it's hardly necessary to describe what a coconut looks like, but it is worth noting that this member of the palm family was probably brought to the Caribbean by the Spanish. In the Caribbean coconut is eaten green or immature. The flesh inside is soft and jelly-like – it's delicious. Coconut is used in numerous dishes as a flavouring, as you may notice from my recipes.

The liquid inside the coconut is known as coconut water and is a delicious drink. One of the best memories I have of drinking coconut water is when I was in Grenada. I was lying on a golden beach when I heard a man's voice singing this calypso . . .

Coconut water,
Sweet as your daughter,
Coconut water,
Coconut

Irresistible! I had to buy one of the big green coconuts he was selling and, boy, was the water sweet as I drank it straight from the shell. Some people drink coconut water as a remedy for kidney problems. Coconut water is not to be confused with coconut milk, which is water and grated coconut squeezed through a sieve.

The best way to get the water out is to pierce the three indentations at the top of the nut and pour it out. Then crack open the shell with a small hammer to get at the flesh.

Coconut Cream

2 fresh coconuts   275 ml (½ pt) cow's milk

Finely grate the coconut. Heat the milk (don't allow to boil) and pour over the grated coconut. Leave to stand for 20 minutes, then sieve through a piece of muslin extracting as much liquid as possible.

Keep chilled in a sealed container and use as a topping or flavouring for desserts and curries. It's also delicious in cocktails or coffee.

Golden Apple

Sometimes known as a pomsitea, this egg-shaped fruit turns from green to yellow as it ripens. Inside is a large seed which has root-like shoots radiating out from it. The flesh is very sweet and makes excellent jam.

There is a lovely traditional 'Anansi the spider man' story, in which Anansi finds pomsiteas so irresistible that he tries to steal them from Kisander the cat's tree. I find them irresistible too!

Granadilla

Also known as barbadine, this fruit has yellow-green, deeply lined skin. It is about 20 cm (8 inches) long and has a lovely acid taste.

Granadilla Sherry Dessert

1 granadilla	50 ml (2 fl oz) sweet sherry
50 g (2 oz) sugar	¼ teaspoon grated nutmeg

Scoop out the fruit. Add sugar and blend well, adding the sherry and nutmeg. Chill well and serve in individual glasses topped with coconut cream.

Guava

A very nutritious yellow round fruit 4–7 cm (1½–3 inches) in diameter. Inside the thick edible skin is the soft pink flesh, which contains dozens of tiny seeds, which are rich in iron. Guava is mainly made into jelly but I love it fresh, skin, seeds and all. It is also available tinned.

Guava Jelly

1 kg (2½ lb) ripe guavas
1 litre (1¾ pt) water

1 kg (2¼ lb) sugar
juice of 3 limes

Wash and slice the guavas. Place them in a large saucepan with the water and boil for about 30 minutes. Strain the fruit through a sieve or a piece of muslin and discard the pulp. Pour the juice back into the saucepan and add the sugar and lime juice. Boil the mixture until it begins to bubble. Allow the mixture to cool, transfer to jam jars and seal.

Guinep

This is a round, green, rough-skinned fruit that grows in grape-like bunches. Inside is one large seed surrounded by pink flesh, which tastes similar to lychees.

Lime

A small, round, green citrus fruit with a sharp refreshing taste. Excellent in cocktails and punches or for adding zest to fish and pancakes. Only buy them when green; if they are yellow they are overripe and about to go off.

Limeade

250 g (9 oz) sugar
1.2 litres (2 pt) water
juice of 4 limes

dash of Angostura bitters
1 lime, sliced, to garnish

Mix sugar with one cup of water and warm till melted. Allow to cool then pour into a large jug and add the lime juice, the rest of the water, bitters and crushed ice. Serve garnished with slices of lime.

Mammy Apple

Mammy apples are a round, thick, rough, brown-skinned fruit. The orange-coloured flesh contains a few seeds and is best stewed or preserved.

Mango

What can I say about the mango! It's probably the West Indians' most favourite fruit; even calypsos are sung about it.

There are many varieties throughout the Caribbean, some round, some oval, some kidney-shaped with tough green, red, orange or yellow skin. Inside is a large stone which is difficult to remove.

Mangoes vary in size, taste and texture. The better varieties are called Julie, Peter, Gordon and Bombay. All mangoes should be eaten soft and ripe. If you are unfamiliar with mango the best way to eat one is to cut four downward slits through to the large central stone, pull off the skin one section at a time and get stuck in. It's a bit messy but the more juicy the mango, the sweeter it is.

Mango Fool

4 ripe mangoes   275 ml (½ pt) double cream
4 level tablespoons castor sugar

Peel the mangoes with a sharp knife and remove the flesh from the large hairy stones. Purée until smooth, add the sugar and cream and whip again until thick and well blended.

Spoon into glasses and chill until ready to serve with crisp almond or chocolate wafers.

Ortanique

This citrus fruit is a Jamaican invention. It's slightly larger than a tangerine and has thin orange skin. Inside is a sweet orange flesh which can be eaten as it is or made into marmalade.

Pawpaw

A smooth-textured fruit about the size of a small melon. The skin is greenish yellow and the orange flesh covers many black seeds.
Pawpaw is ripe when the skin is yellow and soft. Cut into sections, remove the seeds and serve chilled or in fruit salads. The pawpaw has medicinal properties and the unripe fruit is sometimes used in the treatment of dyspepsia.

Pineapple

A native of Guyana, the pineapple is normally eaten fresh cut into slices, with ice cream or as a garnish for cocktails. Pineapple is also excellent in savoury dishes to which it adds a distinctive flavour. Fresh pineapple should give off a delicious aroma. Test for ripeness by pulling off one of the top leaves. It should come away easily.

Pineapple Fritters

1 pineapple
2 tablespoons sugar

dash of Angostura bitters
batter (prepared in the usual way)

Cut pineapple into slices and trim off skin. Sprinkle with the sugar and bitters and leave for 15 minutes. Dip the pineapple in batter and deep fry until golden. Serve as a dessert topped with icecream.

Pomerac

These are deep red pear-shaped fruits with white flesh. They are about 3–5 cm (1–2 inches) long.

Sapodilla

A small, oval, reddish-brown fruit with sweet brown flesh. Sometimes called a naseberry. It has a taste similar to that of dates. The bark of the sapodilla tree is used for making chewing gum. Best eaten as they are or added to fruit salads.

Shaddock

A citrus fruit also known as forbidden fruit or pomelo. It looks like a large rough-skinned grapefruit. The flesh is pale yellow or pink. Eat as you would a grapefruit.

Shaddock Starter   *Serves 2*

1 shaddock
2 tablespoons dark brown sugar
  or honey

Cut the shaddock in two and sprinkle with brown sugar. Place under a hot grill for about five minutes. Decorate with a cherry and serve.

Sorrel

When the flowers of the sorrel wither they leave a fleshy red sepal and it is these that are used to make a popular and delicious drink. In Trinidad we drink it at Christmas time and there is always a jug ready for Christmas visitors. If you're using fresh sorrel only use the sepals and not the seeds. Sorrel can be bought dried, in which case it is already seeded.

Sorrel Drink

500 g (18 oz) sorrel sepals
1 bayleaf
piece of dried orange peel
6 cloves

1.5 litres (2½ pt) boiling water
500 g (18 oz) sugar
½ teaspoon vanilla flavouring
2 tablespoons rum

Put the washed sorrel into a large bowl with the bayleaf, orange peel and cloves. Boil the water, pour into the bowl, cover and leave to soak overnight. Strain the liquid into a jug and stir in the sugar, vanilla flavouring and rum. Store in bottles. Serve with ice.

Soursop

A large heart-shaped fruit with green spiky skin. Inside the flesh is white with black seeds. Soursop smells gorgeous and some say the drink made from it has a calming effect on the nerves.

Soursop Frost

1 soursop
1 litre (1¾ pt) water
1 small tin evaporated milk

1 small tin condensed milk
1 drop vanilla flavouring

Peel the soursop, remove the seeds and put in a liquidizer with the water. Blend for about 30 seconds and strain. Discard the pulp.

SOURSOP

Put liquid back in blender, add milk and flavouring then liquidize for a further 30 seconds. Pour into a container and freeze. When set whisk again and return to freezer. Serve with a cherry on top.

Sugar Cane

Strictly speaking sugar cane is not a fruit but it's well worth a mention. It's eaten like candy in the Caribbean and is a favourite with children and, of course, it's also used to make rum. Sugar cane is full of goodness and the juice and pith can be used as an antiseptic for the throat.

Cut into lengths, peel back outer layers and suck out the sweet juice.

Tamarind

Small brown pods about 5–8 cm (2–3 inches) long. The pods contain seeds which are covered with a sticky brown pulp.

Tamarind is used as a flavouring for curries and drinks.

Ugli Fruit

Misshapen citrus fruit with thick gnarled skin. A cross between a tangerine and a grapefruit, the flesh is pinkish and sweet.

Vegetables

Some of the vegetables in this book will be familiar to you, others less so. The following descriptions may help you to find them but don't be afraid to ask in the market place or supermarket. You'll find lots of help and advice, especially in the street markets. Oh, and don't be put off by the look of some of the vegetables; they do look a bit strange but when they are prepared they look fine and taste delicious.

Sweet potato is probably the best-known Caribbean vegetable and it can be found in most markets nowadays. It looks quite strange but it's very easy to prepare and looks fine when cooked. It can be used in place of ordinary potato and makes a pleasant change.

Many people find plantains puzzling because they look like bananas and yet they have to be cooked!

Yams look awful on the market stall but once again don't be put off, and remember you don't have to buy the whole thing, just ask for a small piece to try out.

Root vegetables like yams, sweet potato and dasheen will keep better if stored dry in a cool dark place. Make sure they are not wrinkled and soft when you buy them as they are more nutritious when they are firm and fleshy. It's the same as buying ordinary potatoes really.

Anyway, the following is a description of some of the most popular Caribbean vegetables that can be bought in many shops and markets nowadays. I've also included tips on how to cook them and how to choose the best quality produce when you're out shopping.

Nutritional Value of Vegetables

Caribbean vegetables are very high in vitamins, minerals and fibre as well as being low in harmful fats and chemicals. Here is a list of vegetables along with their nutritional values.

Per 100g (4oz)

Vegetable	Calories	Fat (g)	Protein (g)	Vit. C (mg)	Vit. A (mcg)	Calcium (mg)	Iron (mg)	Carbohydrate (g)
Bhaji	42	0.8	3.8	65	1600	313	5.6	7.4
Black eye peas or Cow peas	341	1.2	24.1	3	10	77	7.2	60.7
Bread fruit	81	0.5	1.3	29	—	27	1.9	20.1
Cassava	132	0.4	1.0	19	—	40	1.4	32.8
Christophene or Cho-cho	31	0.3	0.9	20	5	12	0.7	7.7
Dasheen	92	0.2	1.6	7	5	96	1.2	22.4
Eddoe (Coco)	92	0.2	1.6	7	5	97	1.5	23.1
Melongene	27	0.3	1.0	5	$\frac{i}{m}$	23	0.8	6.3
Okra	42	0.2	2.2	29	100	78	1.1	9.7
Patechoi	26	0.3	1.7	32	—	136	1.5	54.0
Pawpaw	28	0.1	0.8	36	—	41	0.3	6.9
Pigeon peas or Gungo peas	118	0.6	7.0	49	20	35	1.7	21.7
Plantain (green)	132	0.1	1.2	28	380	8	0.8	32.3
(yellow)	122	0.3	1.0	20	175	8.7	0.9	32.3
Pumpkin	30	0.2	0.6	15	920	19	0.5	7.6
Spinach or Callaloo	19	0.2	1.3	68	860	347	3.9	1.4
Sweet potato	116	0.4	1.4	31	1815	31	1.0	28.6
Tannia	132	0.3	1.8	5	10	14	0.8	30.8
Yam	100	24.3	2.0	3	—	14	1.3	0.6

Bhaji

Bhaji is a leaf vegetable rich in vitamins, iron and calcium. It looks like spinach but the leaves are much smaller and coarser with a pinkish line running through them.

It's cooked in the same way as spinach or fried as below.

Fried Bhaji

1 onion, chopped	500 g (18 oz) bhaji
1 clove garlic, chopped	20 g ($\frac{1}{2}$ oz) coconut cream
2 tablespoons vegetable oil	salt and pepper to taste

Fry the onion and garlic together until brown. Add the washed and chopped bhaji. Stir in the coconut cream and seasoning, cover and allow to simmer gently in its own juices for about five minutes. Take off the lid and continue cooking until all the liquid is gone.

Black Eye Peas

Sometimes known as cow peas, these are small white peas with black eyes and are sold dried. They need to be washed and then boiled until soft. Great cold in salads or cooked up with rice (see page 44).

Bread fruit

These are large round fruits which were introduced to the islands by the famous Captain Bligh. They are approximately 20–25 cm (8–10 inches) in diameter with a rough green skin. Look for ones that are firm and heavy and avoid those that are soft with brown skins as they will be too ripe. Even though it's called 'fruit' it is savoury with a nutty flavour and can be used instead of potatoes. Breadfruit can be served boiled, roasted, fried or even barbecued.

To boil: peel, cut into slices and boil in salted water for 15 to 20 minutes.

To fry: boil first then cut into chips and fry in hot oil until golden brown.

To roast: bake whole in skin for about 30–45 minutes in a medium oven. When cooked carefully peel off skin (it'll be hot so use an oven glove to hold it). Cut in half and take out the middle bit, slice and serve with butter.

To barbecue: peel and cut into large pieces and toast on a skewer over the charcoal until dark brown.

breadfruit

Mashed Breadfruit

1 breadfruit	salt to taste
water for boiling	100 ml (4 fl oz) milk
25 g (1 oz) margarine	50 g (2 oz) grated cheese

Peel the breadfruit, remove the heart and cut into small pieces. Cook in boiling water for 20 minutes. Drain and mash, add margarine, salt and milk. Put into an ovenproof dish, sprinkle the cheese on top and grill until brown.

Cassava

A long brown root vegetable that is rarely found fresh in markets. There are two types of cassava, bitter and sweet. The bitter variety, which is poisonous unless prepared very carefully, is used mainly for making flour. The method of making cassava flour and bread was developed by the Arawak Indians and is still used today. The sweet type is not poisonous and is eaten as a vegetable as well as being used for making bread and puddings.

Sweet cassava has to be peeled, cut up, boiled in salted water and the long central cord removed before serving with butter. Alternatively it can be bought frozen or in tins. Serve as a main vegetable with meat or fish.

Christophene

Also known as cho-cho and chayote. This vegetable looks like a large pear with rough greenish-cream skin. The flesh is white and resembles that of a marrow. Christophene can be cooked with or without the skin, but remember to remove the stone first. It has to be boiled or fried before it can be stuffed with meat or fish and baked in the oven. Peel, rinse, cut into quarters and cook in slightly salted boiling water until tender.

Stuffed Cho-Cho   *Serves 2*

1 christophene	170 g (6 oz) tomatoes
1 onion, chopped	250 g (9 oz) cod, cooked and
2 tablespoons vegetable oil	flaked
thyme, salt and pepper to taste	50 g (2 oz) grated cheese

Wash and halve the christophene then carefully scoop out the flesh. Fry onions in the oil until brown and add the christophene. Stir in the seasoning and continue frying until brown. Add the tomatoes and fish, cook for a few more minutes. Now put the mixture back into the half skins and place in a medium oven, 325°F (160°C, gas mark 3), for about 35 minutes. Sprinkle with grated cheese and serve as a starter or as a main meal with salad.

Dasheen

This large tuberous root vegetable with rough brown skin is a good source of calcium. The flesh has a greyish look unlike similar root vegetables. It can be boiled or baked. Add a dash of lemon juice to the water to retain the colour during cooking.

Peel then cut into pieces and boil in slightly salted water for about 20 minutes. Alternatively boil for 10 minutes and transfer to a hot oven for a further 15 minutes.

Eddoes

Sometimes known as coco, this is also a root vegetable. It has a fine white flesh, is a good substitute for potatoes and can be cooked in the same way. A good tip is to add a dash of lemon juice to the water; this helps to preserve its colour.

Green Bananas

These are ordinary bananas that are used as a vegetable when green. Trim off the ends and boil in their skin for about 20 minutes. Peel off the skin, slice and serve. My favourite way of serving them is to boil them, slice them and fry with onions, tomatoes and thyme.

Melongene

In the Caribbean it is known as melongene or garden egg but elsewhere it's known as aubergine or egg plant.

Can be cooked and eaten with or without the skin. Excellent in stews, stuffed and baked, or fried with onions, tomatoes and thyme.

Okra

Also known as ochro or ladies' fingers. As the name suggests they are like long green fingers. Buy them when they are young and the tips are curved and flexible.

Wash and trim off the stalks. Boil in salted water for about 20 minutes and serve with a knob of butter, or fry with onions, red peppers and tomatoes.

okra

Patechoi

Also known as pak-choi or Chinese cabbage. Looks a bit like an elongated cabbage and is quite common in most markets. A good source of calcium and vitamins and low in calories too! It's a good alternative to regular cabbage and is cooked in the same way.

Patechoi Hash

1 patechoi
1 tin corned beef
2 tablespoons vegetable oil
1 onion, chopped

1 tomato, chopped
thyme, garlic salt and pepper to
   taste

Wash and chop up the patechoi and cut the corned beef into chunks. Fry onions and tomatoes in oil until brown. Then stir in the corned beef and seasoning. Finally add the patechoi and stir-fry for about 5 more minutes. Serve on a bed of boiled rice.

Pawpaw

Sometimes known as papaya this delicious fruit looks like a small melon. When green it is used as a vegetable when ripe it turns yellow and is eaten as a fruit.

To cook as a vegetable, peel the skin and take out the seeds. Cut into pieces and place in boiling salted water until soft. Strain and serve with a knob of butter and decorate with a sprinkling of paprika and chopped chives.

Pigeon or Gungo Peas

Can be bought either fresh or dried. Fresh they are sold in their pods, which are about 5–7 cm (2–3 inches) long and are green in colour. The dried peas are brown and sold loose.

If you buy fresh pigeon peas, remove from the pods, wash and drop them into boiling salted water for about 25 minutes. The dried version must be soaked overnight before cooking, or if you have no time for that a good tip is to add a teaspoon of baking powder to the water, this will soften the peas much quicker. Drain and serve with butter and a sprinkling of chopped mint. Alternatively, don't drain away the water but add a chopped onion, a diced tomato, a clove of garlic, black pepper, a knob of butter, a little coconut cream and a chopped rasher of bacon. Simmer for 5–10 minutes. Delicious served with green bananas, dasheen and a meat dish.

Plantain

Plantains look like large bananas and are in fact part of the same family. However, they cannot be eaten raw and have to be cooked. Buy when ripe but don't buy overripe ones that are brown and soft: look for firm ones to get the best results.

Plantain is one of my favourite vegetables and is extremely versatile; most of the islands in the Caribbean use plantains in their own special way. They can be boiled, mashed and made into dumpling-like balls called Foo-foo to serve in soups. Or they can be mashed, spiced with cinnamon wrapped in banana leaves and boiled to make a dish known as Conkie.

My favourite way of cooking plantain is to simply peel them, cut into slices and fry in oil until brown.

If you're going to boil them, trim off the ends and cook them in their skins to retain the colour and texture. When boiled peel off the skin, slice and serve.

Plantain Crisps

2 plantains (under ripe ones)
enough oil to deep fry

Peel the plantains and cut into thin slices. Deep fry until golden brown. Shake off excess oil, cool and serve as snacks for kids or at parties.

Pumpkin

These are large and melon-shaped with dark green mottled skin and bright yellow flesh, distantly related to the marrow.

To cook pumpkin, peel, remove the seeds, cut into chunks and boil for 15 minutes. Alternatively deep fry until golden brown or bake whole in its skin for about 50 minutes.

I like it best in soup.

Pumpkin Soup   *Serves 6*

1 kg (2¼lb) pumpkin
2.5 litres (4 pt) water
1 ham bone or pigtail
1 chicken stock cube
1 chopped onion
pinch grated nutmeg

1 clove garlic, crushed
1 grated carrot
25 g (1 oz) coconut cream
salt and pepper to taste
1 bayleaf
parsley and thyme to taste

Peel and dice the pumpkin and put into a large saucepan with the water. Add the ham bone or pigtail and bring to the boil, lower heat and simmer for 25 minutes. Stir in the rest of the ingredients and continue to simmer for a further 15 minutes. Remove from heat and allow to cool, then take out the ham bone or pigtail and bayleaf. Pour into a blender or food processor and blend until smooth. Serve cold with cream or hot with a spinkling of parsley.

Spinach or Callaloo

Spinach or callaloo is the basis of some of the most popular Caribbean dishes. (Don't get confused, callaloo is also the name of the dish as well as the vegetable.) Spellings and recipes differ from island to island. In Trinidad we cook callaloo at Christmas or on special occasions. My mum's callaloo recipe is terrific. It always evokes happy memories of many family gatherings and I'd love to share it with you.

Callaloo

Mammy's Callaloo

500 g (18 oz) spinach
1 chilli pepper (optional)
150 g (5 oz) pigtail or bacon
1 onion, chopped
25 g (1 oz) coconut cream
500 ml (18 fl oz) water
25 g (1 oz) butter or margarine

150 g (5 oz) ochros
1 medium-size crab or 150 g (5 oz) frozen crab meat
1 clove garlic, crushed
thyme to taste
vestin (monosodium glutamate – MSG)

Soak the pigtail overnight. Scald and clean the crab. Wash and trim spinach and ochros.

Put all the ingredients except the butter into a large saucepan and simmer for 40 minutes. Add butter and swizzle with a whisk to break up ingredients. If crab is still whole break into pieces so everyone gets a share. A really scrummy traditional dish!

Sweet Potato

This highly nutritious root vegetable which is full of vitamins and minerals is perfect for both sweet and savoury dishes. It is pink in colour and comes in all shapes and sizes. A good tip when buying is to scratch the skin, if the flesh is white or pale yellow it's O K. If it's brown or grey, leave well alone. Sweet potato can be cooked in just about any way imaginable, boiled, fried, roast, barbecued over or in an open fire (which brings out the nutty flavour). It can also be made into pies, candied or puréed.

No matter which way you're going to cook sweet potato, always boil or parboil in the skin first.

To boil, scrub thoroughly and put in boiling salted water for 20 minutes, then peel off the skin to serve.

To fry, boil in skin as above, peel, slice and fry in shallow oil until golden.

To bake or barbecue, parboil first then roast for approximately 25 minutes.

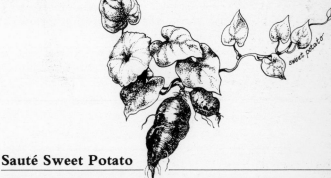

sweet potato

Sauté Sweet Potato

500 g (18 oz) sweet potato   or 150 g (5 oz) breadcrumbs
1 egg   oil to fry
150 g (5 oz) fresh grated coconut

Scrub and boil the potatoes, peel and slice. Beat egg and dip slices of potato in it, cover in grated coconut or breadcrumbs. Fry until golden. Serve with meat or fish or as a vegetarian dish.

Tannia

A long, hairy, dark brown tuber similar to dasheen. It is cooked in the same way.

Tannia Cakes

250 g (9 oz) tannia	salt and pepper to taste
1 tablespoon self-raising flour	oil to fry

Peel the tannia and wash thoroughly, then grate finely. Add flour and seasoning and mix together well. Drop spoonfuls of the mixture into very hot oil in a frying pan and fry until golden. Serve at once with meat or fish.

Yam

Large, brown, hairy-skinned tubers that taste very similar to potatoes when cooked. You might see several varieties of yam on sale in the market and the flesh is usually white or yellow. Don't feel as if you have to buy the whole yam – you can just have a small piece. Always ask to see the yam cut open before buying and if it's brown or bruised inside choose another. Like potatoes, the texture differs depending on the variety: hard or soft, yellow or white. It's always best to ask advice when buying. Hard yams are best used in soups and stews and the soft ones are more suitable to serve as a vegetable with meat and fish.

To cook, peel the skin (this will leave a starchy residue, it's harmless and rinses off). Cut into pieces and boil for 20 minutes in water to which a dash of lemon juice has been added. Serve with butter or mash with a little milk and butter.

Cheesey Yam

250 g (9 oz) yam	50 ml (2 fl oz) milk
150 g (5 oz) grated cheese	salt and black pepper to taste
1 egg	

Peel and boil the yam. Mash and mix in beaten egg, seasoning and cheese leaving a little aside. Place the mixture in an ovenproof dish, sprinkle the remaining cheese on top and put in a medium oven, 350°F (170°C, gas mark 3), for 10 to 15 minutes.

Herbs & Spices

Many herbs and spices were brought to the islands by the Spanish, Portuguese and English from all over the world. The Indians and the Chinese who settled in the islands also contributed their traditional herbs and spices to Caribbean cuisine. Many are now grown there in abundance and exported all over the world. Grenada is known as 'Spice Island', and when I went there I understood why, I could smell the rich aroma of nutmeg, cinnamon, mace and cloves in the air.

Spices are a very important part of Caribbean cookery and are used creatively in all forms of food including drinks, cakes, sweets and puddings as well as meat and fish dishes. Thyme, peppers, allspice and bayleaf are just a few of the herbs and spices found in every Caribbean kitchen. All the herbs and spices listed below can be easily obtained in shops and supermarkets.

Allspice

Closely related to the bayleaf and clove, the dried berries of this useful spice can be used in soups, stews and meat dishes. It is also known as pimento, Jamaican pepper or toute-épice. The best way I can think of to describe the taste is that of cinnamon, cloves and nutmeg all mixed together. Allspice can also be used in pickles, drinks and cakes.

Bayleaf

Aromatic leaf of the bay tree, usually sold dried. Useful in a whole range of savoury dishes. Also adds a distinctive flavour to drinks.

Benne

The seeds are used to flavour cakes and biscuits.

Capsicum

A mixture of sweet and hot peppers used as a flavouring in hot sauces.

Cayenne Pepper

Very hot, ground red pepper used in meat and fish dishes and curries.

Chilli

An extremely hot pepper used for making very strong 'Hot Pepper Sauce' which is sold in bottles and is either used as a condiment at the table or added to many dishes to give a real kick to them.

Chives

Best used fresh as a garnish on salads and soups or cooked in sauces and omelettes to add flavour.

Cinnamon

This is the spicy bark of the cinnamon tree which was brought from the East Indies in the 1700s. Used in sweets, puddings and porridge and can be also used as a flavouring for drinks.

Available as sticks or ground.

Cloves

Dried unopened buds which are used to add spice to cakes, drinks and to bring out the flavour of ham.

Coriander

Small seeds used as a flavouring in curries.

Cumin

A main constituent of curry powder, it can in fact be used alone as an alternative to curry powder. I personally use a little whenever I'm cooking chicken.

Curry Powder

A mixture of herbs and spices probably introduced to the Caribbean by the English. Due to the large Asian population in the Caribbean, curry has become a well-known and accepted part of our cuisine.

Curry powder varies quite a bit in strength and flavour depending on where you buy it. There are hot, medium and mild curry powders. I test before buying by smelling or trying a taste on the end of my finger.

Essences and Flavourings

Essences are widely used as flavouring for cakes, sweets and drinks. They are usually sold in liquid form in small bottles. Vanilla flavouring is very popular; so are almond and orange essences.

Garlic

Well-known strong-flavoured herb, excellent in meat and fish dishes.

Ginger

The root of the ginger plant was introduced to the Caribbean by the Spanish. Nowadays the best ginger is grown in the West Indies. It can be used fresh or powdered. It's particularly good in pork dishes but is also excellent in cakes and puddings. Trinidad is famous for its ginger beer, which is very popular there at Christmas time.

Ginger also has medicinal properties and is the basis for many air and sea sickness remedies. I found ginger tea a saviour when I was pregnant especially when I was suffering from morning sickness.

Mace

Mace is the outer covering of nutmeg and is used for flavouring cakes and puddings.

nutmeg and mace

Monosodium Glutamate (MSG)

Sounds very modern but has been used by the Chinese for centuries. It is the result of the acid hydrolysis of soya beans or seaweed. MSG is a naturally formed product and although totally harmless it has been known to cause some people headaches so use sparingly. It looks like fine crystals and is used to enhance the flavour of many savoury dishes.

Nutmeg

A nut which when ground is used to flavour cakes, drinks and sweets. Best bought whole and grated when needed. This preserves the aroma. It is popular throughout the world and is exported by several Caribbean islands, in particular Grenada.

Paprika

A mild spice used to add colour and flavour to many savoury dishes.

Pepper

There are two types of pepper: black, which is the whole berry and has the stronger flavour of the two, is best kept whole and ground when needed, and white, which has the outer bark removed, is best used for garnishing salads and cold dishes.

Soy Sauce

A Chinese sauce used as a condiment or in the cooking of meat and fish. Mainly features in Trinidadian dishes due to the large Chinese population there.

Tabasco

Strongly flavoured sauce made from cayenne peppers, used mainly as a condiment.

Thyme

A shrub mainly grown in Trinidad and probably introduced to the island by the Spanish. The leaves are highly aromatic and are used in most savoury dishes or in stuffings.

Turmeric

This yellow root is similar to ginger. It has a mild taste and is used in curry powder to give flavour and colour.

Rice, Cereals & Pulses

Rice

Rice is the staple diet of the Caribbean and forms the basis of most meals. For recipes in this book requiring rice any good-quality long grain rice will do. I always find it best to soak rice in the water it is to be cooked in for about 2 hours before boiling. This helps to stop it sticking together and also lowers the cooking time.

Rice can be served plain, 'cooked up' with peas (Rice and Peas), or my favourite way, cooked up with grated coconut or grated carrots.

Carrot Rice

200 g (7 oz) long grain rice	25 g (1 oz) coconut cream
500 ml (18 fl oz) water	salt and black pepper to taste
2 large carrots, grated	knob of butter or margarine

Wash the rice and soak in salted water for about 2 hours then add the grated carrots, coconut cream and pepper. Bring to the boil, stir, cover and simmer on a very low heat for 15–20 minutes or until cooked. Stir in a knob of butter or margarine. Serve with meat or fish. I sometimes eat this dish on its own, especially if I'm watching my diet. For Coconut Rice omit carrots and coconut cream and use freshly grated coconut. Cook in the same way.

Black Eye Peas (see p. 30)

Savoury Black Eye Peas

A filling side dish that can be served with your main dish.

200 g (7 oz) black eye peas	25 g (1 oz) coconut cream
575 ml (1 pt) water	1 rasher of bacon, chopped
2 tomatoes, chopped	thyme, salt and pepper to taste
1 medium onion, chopped	

Boil peas until soft and most of the water has evaporated. Add chopped tomatoes, onions, bacon, coconut cream and seasoning. Stir and leave to simmer for about ten minutes.

Pigeon or Gungo Peas

These can be bought either fresh or dried, and are eaten on their own as a side dish or cooked up with rice.

Pigeon Peas and Rice is a special Christmas dish and is also popular in Trinidad at Carnival time. I remember at the age of five getting up at 4 a.m. on 'J'ouvert' morning. I had to shell the pigeon peas out on the gallery for my mum and watch out for the 'Mas' to go past. But all the excitement disappeared when I saw the tall masked figures dressed as monsters, devils and sea creatures coming towards our house to ask for money. I ran away screaming and hid under the bed until they had all gone away.

Cook up Pigeon Peas and Rice   *Serves 6*

500 g (18 oz) pork spare rib or belly	600 ml (25 fl oz) water
salt and pepper to taste	oil to fry
1 clove garlic, chopped	1 tablespoon sugar
1 onion, chopped	25 g (1 oz) coconut cream
1 sprig thyme	500 g (18 oz) rice
1 chilli pepper	
1 kg (2¼ lb) fresh pigeon peas or 500 g (18 oz) dry weight gungo peas	

Wash, cut up and season the pork with salt, garlic, pepper, onion, thyme and chilli pepper and leave to marinate for about 1 hour. Shell the pigeon peas (soak overnight if dried) and cook in water until tender. In a large saucepan heat the oil with the sugar until almost burning. Remove meat from marinade and brown in oil and sugar, stirring well. Lower heat, cover and cook for about 30 minutes adding a little water if necessary. Stir in the cooked peas (with the water they were cooked in) the marinade, coconut cream and washed rice and simmer until all the water has evaporated and the rice is cooked (about 30 minutes). Serve with a tomato salad.

Red Beans

Also known as kidney beans or red peas, they are very popular and can be served alone or mixed with rice. Normally sold dried or in tins, the dried variety must be boiled then simmered to remove the poisonous toxin they contain. Cook and serve separately or add to soups and stews. Red beans are a popular traditional part of the main Sunday meal.

Red Beans

250 g (9 oz) red beans
250 g (9 oz) pigtail or bacon
750 ml (1¼ pt) water
1 tomato, chopped
thyme
1 chilli pepper or ¼ teaspoon
chilli powder

1 onion, chopped
1 clove garlic, crushed
250 g (2 oz) coconut cream
salt to taste

Wash and soak the beans overnight in the water. Soak the pigtail or bacon overnight to get rid of excess salt, drain and rinse. Add pigtail or bacon to the beans and bring to the boil then simmer till tender. Add all other ingredients and simmer for 15 minutes. Serve as a side dish.

Red Beans and Rice

Cooked as above but in addition you will need
500 g (18 oz) rice soaked in
 750 ml (1¼ pt) water

When the beans and pigtail or bacon are cooked and all the
seasonings are added, stir in the rice and the water it was soaking
in and simmer for a further 25 minutes or until the water has
evaporated. Finally stir in a knob of butter or margarine. Serve
with salad or meat dishes.

Split Peas

Small yellow peas which are sold dried. They can be made into an
East Indian dish called Dal Puri or cooked and added to rice, but
the most popular way of eating them is in Split Pea Soup.

Split Pea Soup   *Serves 4*

250 g (9 oz) split peas	garlic, thyme, bayleaf
500 g (18 oz) stewing lamb	6 dumplings (see p. 47)
2 litres (3½ pt) water	1 onion
250 g (9 oz) yam	50 g (2 oz) coconut cream
250 g (9 oz) dasheen	black pepper and salt to taste

Wash the split peas and meat and put in a large saucepan with 1
litre (1¾ pt) of water. Bring to the boil, lower heat and simmer
until the meat is tender (35–40 min). Peel, wash and dice yam and
dasheen, add to soup along with rest of the water and all the other
ingredients.
    Simmer for a further 30 minutes. Serve as a meal in itself.

Macaroni Pie

We have this as a side dish, along with meat and vegetables, as
part of a meal.

500 g (18 oz) macaroni	150 g (5 oz) cheese, grated
2 eggs, beaten	50 g (2 oz) margarine
50 ml (2 fl oz) milk	

Cook the macaroni and drain. Stir in the margarine, milk, eggs
and most of the cheese. Pour into an oven dish and sprinkle the
remaining cheese on top. Bake in a medium hot oven, 375°F
(190°C, gas mark 4), for 25 minutes. Serve hot.

Cornmeal

Cornmeal is ground corn and it is used in a variety of ways by Caribbean cooks. It can be made into porridge (or 'Pap' as we say), dumplings, puddings or bread. It is also used for making a delicious dish called Coo-Coo which is also known as Fungi.

When I asked my father what was his favourite West Indian meal he went into raptures describing Fungi and Salt Fish and Cornmeal Pap which he had as a child in Antigua. Fungi is still a great favourite with Antiguans and is eaten at almost any meal.

Coo-Coo   *Serves 4*

50 g (2 oz) okra, chopped
1 litre (1¾ pt) water
salt to taste

25 g (1 oz) coconut cream
25 g (1 oz) butter or margarine
250 g (9 oz) cornmeal

Boil the water then put in the okra, margarine, coconut cream and salt. Bring to the boil then lower heat and simmer for 15 minutes. Pour out 250 ml of the water and keep. Then on a very low heat gradually add to the okra, the cornmeal and the saved water a little at a time stirring constantly. Keep stirring until smooth and then leave on a low heat to cook for 10 minutes stirring occasionally (the coo-coo must not be too stiff or too soft and runny). When the mixture turns into a ball and leaves the sides of the saucepan, remove from the heat. Spoon out a quarter of the mixture into a greased bowl and rock the bowl from side to side until the coo-coo forms a ball; place this on a plate. Repeat with the rest of the coo-coo for the other servings. Alternatively, put all the coo-coo into one big bowl, shape and cut into four individual servings. Serve with fried fish or meat.

My mother used to always cook this dish for Saturday dinner when I was a child and even now, whenever I visit her on Saturdays, I am disappointed if she does not prepare coo-coo for me.

Cornmeal Dumplings

50 g (2 oz) cornmeal
50 g (2 oz) self-raising flour
50 g (2 oz) margarine

pinch of salt
water

Mix all ingredients together then add a little water at a time to form a stiff dough. Roll into small balls and add to soups or stews.

Dumplings can be made in the same way using only flour, but I always find cornmeal gives them a nicer taste.

Porridge

The porridge eaten in the Caribbean is not only made from cereals but from fruit and vegetables. Porridge was introduced to the Caribbean by the English, but nowadays bears no resemblance to the original. It is eaten for breakfast or last thing at night.

We also refer to porridge as 'Pap' and these recipes were told to me by my father, who remembered them from his childhood and later cooked them for myself and my brothers and sisters.

Cocoa Rice Pap

250 g (9 oz) white rice
500 ml (18 fl oz) water
250 ml (9 fl oz) milk
pinch of nutmeg and allspice

2 drops vanilla flavouring
cloves
sugar to taste
2 tablespoons cocoa

Wash and boil the rice until very soft, add milk, nutmeg, allspice, vanilla flavouring, cloves and sugar and stir. Add the cocoa and simmer for 5 minutes. Serve with a sprinkle of cocoa and nutmeg on top.

Cornmeal Pap

150 g (5 oz) cornmeal
750 ml (1¼ pt) milk
pinch of nutmeg and allspice

drop of vanilla flavouring
sugar to taste

Mix the cornmeal in a little water. Boil the milk and gradually mix in the cornmeal stirring vigorously. Do not allow to get lumpy (my father assures me that this is quite an art). It must not be too runny or too thick. Add spices, flavouring and sugar. Serve with a drop of cold milk on top.

Plantain Porridge

1 litre (1¾ pt) milk
2 firm plantains, grated
cloves, nutmeg, allspice, vanilla
  flavouring

1 tablespoon cornflour
sugar to taste

Mix the grated plantain and milk together and bring to the boil,
lower heat and simmer for about 15 minutes. Mix cornflour with
a little milk and add to the porridge with the sugar, flavouring
and spices, stirring constantly. Delicious served with honey on
top.

Arrowroot Pap

Arrowroot pap is said to be very beneficial to convalescents.

50 g (2 oz) arrowroot
500 ml (18 fl oz) milk
sugar to taste

drop of vanilla flavouring
cinnamon
nutmeg

Mix the arrowroot in a little water until smooth. Boil the milk
and pour in arrowroot, spices and flavouring, stirring constantly,
and cook for 10 minutes. Sprinkle nutmeg on top and serve.

Sweet Potato Porridge

500 g (18 oz) sweet potato
750 ml (1¼ pt) milk
pinch of nutmeg

pinch of allspice
drop of vanilla flavouring
sugar to taste

Peel, wash and grate the sweet potato. Dry in a low oven, 300°F
(148°C, gas mark 2). Boil the milk and gradually mix in the dried
sweet potato, stirring all the time. Simmer for 20 minutes then
add spices and sugar. Serve with a little cold milk on top.

Soups

In the Caribbean, soups are often served as a main meal. They are thick and rich and are made with meat (both fresh and salted), fish and pulses. Cornmeal dumplings are also added to soups along with numerous vegetables such as cho-chos, pumpkin, callaloo, green bananas, yams, in fact just about anything you fancy!

No Caribbean dish is complete without seasoning and soup is no exception. I find fresh thyme really brings out the flavour in soups. We do sometimes serve soups as starters but they are usually the light soups such as Avocado or Lobster Soup or Orange Consommé. Whether you have them as a starter or a main course you will find them all quite exotic and delicious.

Avocado Soup

4 ripe avocados
1 tablespoon lime or lemon
2 tablespoons finely chopped
  chives
150 g (5 oz) cooked crab meat
1 litre (1¾ pt) milk
salt and pepper to taste

Cut the avocados in half and remove the stones. Scoop out the flesh and put in a blender with the lime juice, chives, crab meat, milk and seasoning.

Blend well and chill well before serving with toast fingers covered with melted cheese.

Lobster Soup

1 cooked lobster
1 litre (1¾ pt) chicken stock
1.2 litres (2 pt) milk
4 tablespoons cream
salt and pepper to taste
4 tablespoons sherry
paprika

Shred the lobster meat. Warm the chicken stock and milk slowly and add the lobster. Gently stir in the cream, salt and pepper. Do not allow to boil but simmer gently for 20 minutes, stirring all the time. Before serving add sherry and garnish with paprika.

Orange Consommé

1 400 g (14 oz) tin of beef
  consommé
juice of three oranges

2 cloves
grated orange peel to decorate

Heat the consommé, cloves and juice together and serve hot or
cold garnished with orange peel.

Pineapple Consommé

1 400 g (14 oz) tin of chicken
  consommé
500 ml (18 fl oz) fresh pineapple
  juice

pinch of nutmeg
watercress to garnish

Heat the consommé, juice and nutmeg together and serve hot or
cold garnished with watercress.

Coconut Soup

150 g (5 oz) salt pork
500 g (18 oz) stewing beef
2.5 litres (4½ pt) water
2 small cocos, diced

1 sprig of thyme
525 ml (1 pt) coconut milk
chopped chives or spring onions
salt and pepper to taste

Soak the salt pork overnight. Wash the beef and put in a large
saucepan with the water, cocos and pork and cook till tender.
Then add thyme, chives, coconut milk and seasoning and simmer for 10 minutes. Serve hot.

Man-Soup

My father gave me this Antiguan recipe. He claims that in Antigua, 'Man order it from woman'... a more chauvinist quote I've never heard! According to my father it's supposed to make you strong and virile so it's usually eaten before a competition or if you are planning to make babies!

500 g (18 oz) white fish fillet
250 g (9 oz) peeled, sliced yam
250 g (9 oz) okra, trimmed
3 carrots, chopped
1 sprig thyme
2.5 litres (4½ pt) water
salt and pepper to taste
1 lemon
250 g (9 oz) dasheen or coco peeled & sliced

250 g (9 oz) pumpkin, peeled and chopped
500 g (18 oz) cornmeal (for dumplings)
1 clove garlic
1 chilli pepper
1 teaspoon pimento
1 bayleaf
knob of butter

Wash and clean the fish with lemon. Season with salt, pepper, thyme and garlic, leave to marinate. Put all the vegetables in a large pan with the water and bring to the boil, lower heat and cook for 25 minutes. Make cornmeal dumplings with a pinch of salt and a little water. The mixture should be firm and easily rolled into balls.

Add them to the soup along with the fish, the marinade, chilli pepper, pimento and butter. Leave to simmer for 15 minutes. Serve hot. This recipe serves four people or ONE MAN!

Beef Soup

This is cooked using the same ingredients as fish soup only using braising steak instead of fish. The beef should be cooked with the vegetables.

Mutton and Corn Soup

500 g (18 oz) mutton or lamb
1.5 litres (2½ pt) water
1 onion, chopped
2 cho-chos, chopped
chives

chilli pepper
4 fresh cobs of corn
250 g (9 oz) pumpkin, chopped
parsley

Cut up and remove any excess fat from the mutton. Put in a large saucepan with the water and bring to the boil, skimming off excess fat. Add vegetables and seasonings and cook for a further 30 minutes. Serve hot.

Jamaican Pepperpot Soup

Jamaican Pepperpot Soup and Guyanese Pepper-pot are two completely different dishes and should not be confused. One is a soup the other an extraordinary stew! In fact Pepperpot Soup has the same origins as Pepper-pot but over the years it has gradually changed into soup. It was originally a dish for rich plantation owners. The slaves had their own version made with salt fish.

Nowadays you don't have to be rich or a plantation owner to enjoy this delicious dish.

250 g (9 oz) salt beef or salt pork
1 kg (2¼ lb) stewing steak
3 litres (4 pt) water
500 g (18 oz) callaloo or spinach
24 ochros, chopped
500 g (18 oz) yam, sliced
250 g (9 oz) coco

4 spring onions
1 sprig of thyme
1 clove garlic, chopped
50 g (2 oz) coconut cream
salt and pepper to taste
2 onions

Wash and soak the salt beef or pork for 1 hour then rinse and put in a large saucepan with fresh water and chopped steak. Bring to the boil then lower heat and simmer for 45 minutes. Add callaloo and ochros and continue to simmer for a further 30 minutes. Add the yam, coco, onions, thyme, garlic, coconut cream, salt and pepper and simmer for another 30 minutes. This stew should be rich and thick, serve it hot.

Crab Gumbo   *Serves 4*

50g (2oz) butter or margarine
3 hard-boiled eggs
juice and finely grated rind of 1
  lemon
50g (2oz) flour
1.5litres (2½pt) milk
chives

bayleaf
350g (12oz) crab meat
salt and pepper to taste
4 tablespoons sherry
dash of Angostura bitters
50ml (2floz) cream

Melt the butter and when cool mix with eggs until they are a fine paste. Add lemon juice, rind and flour and mix well. Heat the milk and gradually stir into the egg mixture, make sure there are no lumps. Add chopped chives and bayleaf, return the saucepan to the heat and bring to the boil stirring constantly. Simmer for 6–7 minutes. Add the crab meat, salt and pepper, sherry and bitters and simmer for a further 5 minutes. Serve hot or cold with cream and a sprinkling of chives and paprika.

Salads

Salads play an important part in a West Indian meal and they are varied and spicy. Salads are normally served with the main course and rarely as a meal in themselves but they can be served as a starter.

Cucumber Salad

1 cucumber, peeled
salt and pepper

vinegar
1 chilli pepper (optional)

Wash and slice the cucumber thinly, season with vinegar, chilli, salt and pepper.

Avocado Salad

2 avocados, sliced
juice of 1 lemon
2 tablespoons olive oil

1 teaspoon brown sugar
salt and pepper
4 teaspoons rum (optional)

Mix the lemon juice, olive oil and sugar well with salt and pepper and add rum if desired. Place the avocados on a bed of lettuce and pour on dressing, chill and serve.

Breadfruit Salad

2 tablespoons olive oil
1 tablespoon vinegar
salt and pepper
3 blades chopped chives

1 cooked breadfruit, diced
2 sticks celery, chopped
1 onion, sliced

Mix together the olive oil, vinegar, chives, salt and pepper and pour over chopped breadfruit, onion and celery. Mix well, chill and serve.

Yam can be used for this salad instead of breadfruit.

Mango Salad

2 large unripe mangoes,
  chopped
salt and pepper

2 tablespoons vinegar
1 lettuce, chopped
1 cucumber, sliced

Mix the mangoes and cucumber together, pour on vinegar, salt and pepper and leave to marinate. Serve on a bed of lettuce. This salad goes well with fish dishes.

Antiguan Lobster Salad

4 tablespoons tomato ketchup
4 tablespoons mayonnaise or
  salad cream
juice of 1 orange
juice of 1 lemon
salt and pepper

500 g (18 oz) cooked lobster meat
150 g (5 oz) pineapple, chopped
25 g (1 oz) preserved ginger
4 spring onions, chopped
1 lettuce

Mix the tomato ketchup, mayonnaise or salad cream, orange and lemon juice together. Stir in salt and pepper. Mix together the lobster meat, pineapple, ginger and spring onions and place on a bed of lettuce. Pour on dressing and chill. Serve as a starter.

Vegetable Mayonnaise Salad

4 tablespoons mayonnaise or
  salad cream
2 cooked carrots, diced
1 cooked beetroot, diced

4 cooked potatoes, diced
150 g (5 oz) green peas
black pepper, to taste
paprika, to garnish

Mix all the ingredients together, season with pepper and garnish with paprika. Chill and serve. I love this salad with meat dishes.

Fish

Fish is abundant in the Caribbean and the many varieties that are found in the warm waters have always provided a plentiful source of food for the islands.

Once again each island has its own name for each type of fish. There can even be three or four different names for the same fish on the same island. This can be very confusing so I've tried to give some alternative names and describe each one as best I can.

In the Caribbean fish is sold freshly caught and sometimes still alive and the market place bustles with excitement when the catch arrives. I'll never forget as a five-year-old in Trinidad, running down to the crowded wharf in Marabella with my sister Sandra to buy fresh fish for my mother to cook that evening. We sang all the way there and back. Oh those were such happy days!

In recent years I've noticed that many of the more exotic fish are being exported and sold frozen in specialist fishmongers. I get my fish at Dagons in Brixton market arcade which stocks everything from barracuda to flying fish. They even had a shark on sale there one day, which caused a lot of excitement and attracted a large crowd of onlookers. No doubt they had seen the film *Jaws* and wanted to see the real thing.

Fish can be divided into three types; dark oily fleshed fish, shell fish and white-fleshed fish. The much loved salt fish which is mentioned in many Caribbean dishes is imported salted cod and has been part of Caribbean traditional cuisine since it was brought to the islands as a cheap source of protein to feed the slaves. Nowadays salt fish is considered a luxury as it is expensive compared with locally caught fresh fish.

If you can't find the fish specified in the recipes you can use more easily available alternatives. A plain piece of cod seasoned and cooked according to my recipes will at least give the flavour of the Caribbean.

Barracuda

Also known as bechine, this large white-fleshed silver fish grows to about 2 m (6 ft) in length. It has a pointed head and its mouth is lined with razor-sharp teeth. The smaller species of barracuda grows to only about 30 cm (1 ft) and also has white flesh. Barracuda is good steamed or boiled.

Blue Fish

A fat silvery-skinned white-fleshed fish about 30–60 cm (1–2 ft) long. It weighs between 5 and 6 kg (11 and 13 lb). Good filleted and fried or baked whole.

Bonito

Also known as little tunny or spotted tuna. Common in the waters around Tobago. Bonito has silvery-blue skin with dark lines and spots. The flesh is oily and dark and is normally filleted and dried. The roe of the bonito is considered a delicacy.

Butterfish

Also known as palomette, this oval-shaped fish is blue in colour turning to silver along the underside. Inside the mouth is very dark blue. The flesh is white and it is best baked or fried whole.

Carangue

This is a large family of fish which includes cavalli, jacks, horse cavalli and gros yeux. These are the larger of the species, growing to almost a metre in length with greenish-gold skin, a flat face and blunt snout. Round Robin, cigar fish, goggle-eyed jack and big eye are smaller and have a large characteristic eye – hence the name. They are dark silvery-green in colour. The flesh of all these fish is dark and oily.

Cascadura or Cascadou

We have a saying in Trinidad that if you eat cascadou you will return to Trinidad to end your days.

These shellfish inhabit muddy pools and are most common in the fish markets in Trinidad from February to April where they are sold alive. They are about 15 cm (6 inches) long and dark blue grey in colour.

Chip-chip

A tiny shellfish that tastes a little like clam and can be used in chowder in place of clams.

Conch

Most people have seen the large shell of the conch. It is about 25 cm (10 inches) long with a rough cone shape. Native fishermen use the shell as a trumpet to signal that they are returning with their catch.

In the Bahamas the conch is a delicacy.

Crab

There are two types of crab in the Caribbean, the sea crab and the land crab. Land crab has a softer shell and is the best type to use in Callaloo. When I was in Barbados I had the most delicious Crab Back I have ever had, and no wonder since it's a Bajan speciality.

It is usual to prepare crab by boiling it first in salted water before following a particular recipe.

Crayfish

Caribbean crayfish are large and delicious. They look like lobsters with no claws. They taste a bit like lobster too.

Cutlas Fish or Coutelas Fish

Long, tapered, silver-coloured fish. Grows to about 1 metre (3 ft). The flesh is white and very bony, nevertheless it's delicious in soups.

Eel

In the Caribbean there are three kinds of eel: the conger eel, common eel and green moray. They are normally used in soup, the moray being the favourite.

Flying Fish

When I was a child I was travelling by ship near Barbados and I went on deck to see the sun setting. I will never forget the sight of hundreds of silver fish flying through the air above the sea. I thought it was a miracle. It was, of course, a shoal of flying fish, which abound in the waters around Barbados and are a speciality of the island.

The flesh is moist, white and succulent and the Bajans turn it into a gastronomic delight by baking, stuffing, frying, boiling or stewing – in fact preparing it in any way imaginable. And, believe me, it's delicious.

Grouper or Sea Bass

There are three types of grouper: the black grouper, which is, in fact, dark blue or brown with yellow spots and can measure up to 1.5 metres (5 ft) and weigh 50 kg (110 lb); the red grouper, which is large and heavy, growing up to 1 metre (3 ft) and weighing as much as 25 kg (50 lb); and the much smaller spotted grouper, a grey and white fish with red and brown spots. The spotted grouper grows to about 50 cm (20 inches).

All the above fish have white flesh and are excellent to eat. They can be cooked in any way.

Grunt or Gro-gro

White-fleshed fish excellent fried or grilled. There are many different species of grunt so I won't try to describe them all. I am sure your fishmonger will advise on this one.

Herring

Also known as thread herring or harangue. A silver fish with dark blue green markings along it's back. Anything from 2.5 to 30 cm (1 to 12 inches) long, it has dark oily flesh and is best baked or fried.

King Fish

Also known as tassard or mackerel. A large dark grey fish growing to 1.5 metres (5 ft) long and weighing as much as 50 kg (110 lb).

The flesh is white with a dry texture and is best grilled or steamed. It is also sometimes salted and called tasa salle.

Lobster

Lobster needs no description. It is a favourite throughout the Caribbean, where it is cooked in a variety of ways, even curried.

Oyster

In Trinidad oysters can be found on rocks and mangrove roots when the tide goes out. They are smaller and tastier than the more common type.

Pompano

Also known as carangue France or carangue à plume. This solid looking fish has bluish-silvery skin and grows to a length of about 30 cm (12 inches). It has dark oily flesh.

Salmon

Also known as weak fish, sea trout or bangomaree. A long silver fish with white succulent flesh.

Salt Salmon

This is salmon which has been preserved in brine. This method of preserving food started in the days before refrigeration.

Salt salmon is cooked on Good Fridays in olive oil and vinegar.

Salt Fish

This is cod or other firm-fleshed white fish which has been placed in salt to preserve it.

To prepare salt fish wash it well and then place in a saucepan with a slice of lemon peel and plenty of water. Bring to the boil and then throw the water away. Repeat two or three times to remove all the excess salt. Finally break into pieces and fry or use in curry.

Sea Eggs

These are really sea urchins and they are a speciality of Barbados, where they are sautéed with butter and onions. They can also be served raw with lemon juice as an hors d'oeuvre.

Shrimp

These shell-fish are found all over the Caribbean.

Snapper

Also known as red snapper, red fish, pargue, vivenot or jolie-bleu. This large family of fish range in size from 1 to 1.5 metres (3 to 5 ft) in length and weigh from 10 to 20 kg (22 to 44 lb). They are usually pink or red and have white flesh. They can be baked, boiled or steamed.

Shark

Large carnivorous fish varying in size from about 50 cm (15 inches) to several metres long. Its flesh can be tough and is sometimes shredded after cooking. It can be fried or steamed and is excellent in soups and curries.

Spanish Mackerel

A very common fish in the Caribbean. The carite, as it is sometimes known, is a silver mottled fish growing to 1 metre (3 ft) long and weighing up to 10 kg (22 lb). Its white flesh is best boiled or steamed.

White Mullet

A long green-blue fish with dark oily flesh. Can be baked or fried.

As you may well know fish is very good for you. It's rich in vitamins and minerals and low in fat and should form an important part of any balanced diet. I eat fish at least three times a week. The secret of really tasty fish is in the seasoning and method of cooking. My list of essential ingredients for seasoning fish are;

lemon or lime   onion
salt   garlic
black pepper   celery salt
chilli pepper   ginger
vinegar   tomatoes
thyme   MSG

The recipes that follow will use all or a combination of these ingredients. It's also important to marinate the fish in the seasoning for about two hours before cooking to allow the flavour to really soak in. As I explained earlier, if you marinate and cook any fish, even an ordinary plain piece of cod, using these seasonings, it will have the true Caribbean flavour.

A basic sauce that I find goes with most fish dishes is Salamagundy Sauce. Cooks all over the Caribbean have their own way of preparing it. This is my mum's way of cooking Salamagundy Sauce.

Mammy's Salamagundy Sauce

1 tablespoon olive oil
2 onions, chopped
1 red pepper, chopped
1 chilli pepper, chopped
  (optional)
1 tablespoon cornflour or flour

1 400g (14oz) tin of tomatoes
1 sprig thyme (optional)
150ml (5floz) water
salt and pepper
50g (2oz) margarine

Fry the onions, red pepper and chilli together for 3 minutes. Sprinkle in cornflour and stir well. Add tomatoes, thyme, water, salt and pepper. Simmer for 15 minutes then add margarine and simmer for a further 3 minutes. Serve with fish or vegetable dishes.

Salamagundy
Born on Monday,
Christened on Tuesday,
Married on a Wednesday,
Taken sick on a Thursday,
Worse on a Friday,
Died on a Saturday,
That's the end of Salamagundy!

This is a rhyme my sisters and I used to say when we played the Salamagundy game in Trinidad.

I was amazed to see Salamagundy Fish on a Portuguese menu when I visited the Algarve. I shouldn't have been so surprised since Portugal and the Caribbean do have very strong links. In fact, while I was in Faro, the main town of the Algarve, the architecture reminded me very much of the West Indies. The flavour of some of the Portuguese dishes was also very similar to many Caribbean dishes.

Fried Blue Fish

250 g (9 oz) blue fish fillet or cutlets (cod, coley or haddock will do)
½ lemon or lime
1 chilli pepper, chopped (remember to wash your hands after chopping)
2 tablespoons vinegar
1 teaspoon thyme
2 cloves garlic, crushed
celery salt to taste
1 pinch ginger
1 teaspoon MSG
black pepper
3 tablespoons flour
3 tablespoons oil to fry
1 onion, chopped
2 tomatoes, chopped
25 g (1 oz) margarine
150 ml (5 fl oz) water

Clean and wash the fish. Squeeze the lemon over it and set aside for about 20 minutes. Rinse the fish and place in a deep bowl with pepper, vinegar, thyme, garlic, celery salt, ginger and MSG and mix thoroughly using your hands. Leave to marinate in a cool place for up to 2 hours, then remove the fish and put the bowl of marinade aside.

Grind a little black pepper into the flour and coat the fish, place in a hot frying pan and fry till golden. Use a fresh pan to fry the onions and tomatoes in margarine for 2 to 3 minutes. Stir in a teaspoon of flour to thicken and add the marinade along with the water. Stir and leave to simmer for 5 minutes. Arrange the fish on a hot dish, cover with sauce and serve with rice or vegetables.

Baked Crab
Serves 4

4 crabs, boiled
150 g (5 oz) breadcrumbs
2 tomatoes, chopped
1 onion, chopped
1 pinch thyme
1 pinch cayenne pepper

celery salt
pepper to taste
1 beaten egg
25 g (1 oz) butter or margarine
50 g (2 oz) grated cheese

Open the crabs and remove the eggs and gall and clean the shells thoroughly. Take out all the meat, including claws, and flake. Mix with all the ingredients except the cheese and spoon back into the shells. Sprinkle the cheese on top and place in the oven at 350°F (180°C, gas mark 4) for 15 minutes. Serve as a starter or as a main course with salad or vegetables.

Crab Back

6 crabs, boiled
1 onion, chopped
1 tablespoon freshly chopped
  chives
50 g (2 oz) butter or margarine

1 tablespoon Worcestershire
  sauce
salt and pepper to taste
150 g (5 oz) dried breadcrumbs
dash of hot pepper sauce
  (optional)

Open the crabs and discard the gall, wash shells thoroughly. Remove all the meat from the claws and body and flake. Fry the onions and chives in butter until golden brown. Add the crab meat, Worcestershire sauce, salt and pepper. Mix well, spoon the mixture into shells and sprinkle with breadcrumbs. Place in a preheated oven, 400°F (200°C, gas mark 6), for 10 minutes. Serve with salad or vegetables.

Crab Soufflé

50 g (2 oz) butter	salt and pepper to taste
25 g (1 oz) flour	3 eggs
300 ml (11 fl oz) milk	3 tablespoons sherry
pinch of grated nutmeg	500 g (18 oz) crab meat
pinch cayenne pepper	50 g (2 oz) breadcrumbs

On a low heat melt the butter and gradually stir in the flour. Remove from the heat and slowly stir in the milk, nutmeg and seasonings. Return to low heat and stir constantly until thick, then simmer very gently for 5 minutes. Leave to cool. Separate out the egg yolks, beat and stir into cooled mixture; add the sherry and crab meat. Stiffly beat the egg whites, add to the mixture and pour into a soufflé dish. Sprinkle the breadcrumbs on top. Bake in the oven, 400°F (200°C, gas mark 6), for 30 minutes. Serve as a starter.

You can use any white flaked fish meat for this recipe. Even salt fish makes a delicious soufflé.

Sauté Conch

250 g (9 oz) conch (squid or octopus will do)	1 onion
1 lemon	vegetable oil to fry
250 ml (9 fl oz) water	salt and chilli pepper to taste
	parsley

Wash the conch and soak in lemon juice for 20 minutes. Drain and put in a saucepan with boiling water and cook for 5 minutes and then drain. Fry the onion in oil until golden brown then add the salt and pepper and the conch. Sauté for 2–3 minutes. Serve on a bed of rice. Garnish with parsley.

Coconut Blue Fish

1 kg (2¼ lb) blue fish (plaice or sole will do)	ginger
salt and pepper to taste	chilli pepper (optional)
½ lemon	150 g (5 oz) butter
1 clove garlic, chopped	250 ml (9 fl oz) coconut milk or coconut cream
celery salt	

Season the fish with the spices, lemon and garlic and leave to marinate. Fry in butter until golden brown then add coconut milk cream and simmer for 5 minutes. Serve with rice.

Caribbean Baked Fish

2 kg (4½ lb) whole fish
ginger
pepper and salt to taste
chilli pepper (optional)
juice of 1 lemon
1 large cucumber, peeled and
 chopped
500 g (18 oz) breadcrumbs

2 onions chopped finely
1 sprig of thyme
parsley, chopped
1 clove garlic, chopped
rind of ½ lemon
3 tablespoons water
100 g (4 oz) butter

Slit open the fish to its tail, clean and wash. Season it with ginger, salt and pepper, chilli and lemon juice and leave it to marinate.

To make the stuffing

Place the cucumber, breadcrumbs, onion, thyme, parsley, garlic, salt and pepper, lemon rind and water in a bowl and blend well together.

Take fish out of marinade and place it on a piece of foil. Fill with the stuffing and skewer together. Put a knob of butter on top and wrap it in foil. Put in a baking dish and bake in a hot oven, 425°F (225°C, gas mark 7) for 40 minutes. Unwrap and bake for a further 5 minutes. Garnish with lemon and parsley, serve hot with vegetables or cold with salad.

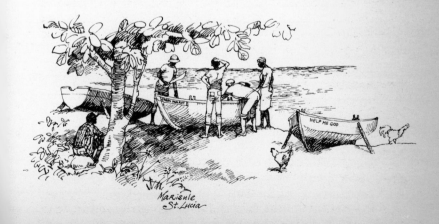

Marisule
St. Lucia

Escovitch Fish

1 kg (2¼ lb) fish fillets (red
  snappers, jacks or plaice)

Sauce
100 ml (4 fl oz) vinegar
chilli peppers
2 onions, chopped

2 bayleaves
1 lime or lemon
salt and pepper to taste
2 cho-chos, peeled and chopped
pinch of allspice
500 ml (18 fl oz) water

Wash and clean the fish and soak in lemon juice for 20 minutes.
Drain and season with salt and pepper.

To make the sauce

Place in a saucepan cho-chos, chilli peppers, bayleaves, onions,
vinegar, allspice and water. Bring to the boil, then simmer for 5
minutes. Grill the fish until brown, place in serving dish and pour
sauce over it. Serve hot or leave to marinate in sauce until cold.

  This is a famous Jamaican dish and is very popular there. It is
usually served at breakfast time with Bakes or Johnny Cakes.
Other islands have their own recipes for this dish. It is sometimes
called Caveached Fish and was introduced into the Caribbean by
both the French and Spanish.

Calypso Salt Fish

250 g (9 oz) salt fish (or kippers)
lemon or orange peel
25 g (1 oz) margarine
1 onion, chopped

1 tomato, chopped
1 tablespoon chives, chopped
black pepper
2 large avocados

Boil the salt fish with a slice of lemon peel for 5–10 minutes,
discard the water and repeat the process to get rid of excess salt.
Flake the fish. Fry the onion and tomato for 3 minutes and add the
fish, chives and pepper. Cook for 5 minutes.

  Halve and peel the avocados and remove the stones. Cut into
slices and mix with the salt fish. Serve on a bed of lettuce
garnished with chives.

  You can substitute ackee for the avocados (use tinned ackee).
Ackee cooked with salt fish is one of Jamaica's favourite dishes.
Unlike avocado, which will taste bitter if cooked, the ackee can
be fried with the salt fish. Salt fish can be served as a starter, in a
salad, as a main dish with yams and green bananas, dumplings
and roast breadfruit or on its own or for breakfast with hot Bakes.

Salt Fish Buljou

When I was in Grenada I was awakened one morning by the most wonderful smell which made me feel instantly hungry. My host was cooking bhaji and salt fish for breakfast. I've cooked it several times but I've never captured the same aroma . . . maybe it was just the Grenadan air!

250 g (9 oz) salt fish	1 clove garlic, chopped
1 piece lemon	black pepper to taste
250 g (9 oz) spinach	2 tablespoons oil to fry
1 onion, chopped	75 g (3 oz) coconut cream
chilli pepper (optional)	

Prepare the salt fish by boiling with a piece of lemon twice and flaking. Wash and chop the spinach. Fry the onion with garlic and seasoning. Add the spinach, salt fish and coconut cream, stirring well. Cover and leave to simmer in its own juice for 10–15 minutes. Then uncover and allow to dry off before serving hot with vegetables . . . delicious.

Spicy Red Snapper

6 small red snappers (trout can be used instead)	1 400 g (14 oz) tin of tomatoes
$\frac{1}{2}$ teaspoon chilli powder	2 cloves garlic, crushed
$\frac{1}{2}$ teaspoon ground nutmeg	juice of 1 lemon
$\frac{1}{2}$ teaspoon ginger	salt and pepper
$\frac{1}{4}$ teaspoon ground cumin	4 tablespoons oil to fry
4 tablespoons flour	1 tablespoon chopped parsley
2 onions, sliced	
50 g (2 oz) butter	

Mix together all the spices and rub into the fish. Leave to marinate. Fry the sliced onions in butter until tender, add the tomatoes and their juice, crushed garlic, lemon juice and seasoning. Simmer gently for about 30 minutes.

Remove the fish from the marinade. Grind a little black pepper into the flour and coat the fish. Heat the oil in a frying pan and brown the floured fish on both sides. (This might have to be done in several batches.)

Lay the browned fish in an ovenproof dish, pour the tomato sauce over it and cover with foil. Bake in a medium oven, 375°F (190°C, gas mark 5), for about 20 minutes. Serve hot with Carrot Rice (see page 43), yams, plantains and green bananas.

Curried Shrimps

500 g (18 oz) shrimps (frozen
  prawns will do)
1 onion, chopped
1 clove garlic, chopped
1 tablespoon oil to fry
1 tablespoon cumin
2 tablespoons curry powder

1 tomato, chopped
1 chilli pepper
50 g (2 oz) coconut cream
salt and pepper to taste
250 ml (9 fl oz) water
knob of butter

Peel the shrimps, wash and drain. Fry the onion and garlic in oil
and add the shrimps. Stir in the cumin and curry powder, add the
tomatoes, chilli pepper, coconut cream, salt and pepper and
simmer for 2 minutes. Pour in the water and allow to boil. Add
butter and simmer for 10–15 minutes. Serve with rice or green
bananas, yams and plantains.

You can also prepare salt fish curry, crab curry and lobster
curry in the same way.

Bajan Flying Fish

4 flying fish, filleted (whiting
  will do)
juice of 2 lemons
ginger
salt and pepper to taste
thyme
garlic

1 egg
garlic salt
chilli pepper
2 tablespoons milk
50 g (2 oz) flour
oil to fry

Wash and clean the fish with lemon and season with ginger, salt,
pepper, thyme and garlic. Leave to marinate in the lemon juice
for 10 minutes. Place on kitchen tissue to absorb moisture. Beat
the egg with the garlic salt, chilli pepper and milk. Dip the fish
into the mixture, coat in flour and black pepper, then fry in hot oil
until golden brown.

Serve with Salamagundy Sauce (see page 63) on a bed of rice or
with vegetables.

Bajan Steamed Flying Fish

4 flying fish (whiting or herring
  will do)
1 lemon or lime
salt and pepper to taste
chilli pepper (optional)

1 garlic clove, chopped
chives, chopped
2 sliced tomatoes
2 sliced onions
knob of butter

Clean and wash the fish. Season with lemon juice, salt, pepper, chilli, garlic and chives and leave for 20 minutes. Place in a large frying pan with the marinade and add the sliced onions, tomatoes and knob of butter. Cover and steam for 20–30 minutes.*

If you can get hold of some barracuda you can cook it in the same way. It's wonderful.

*N.B. Can be microwaved on high for 5–6 minutes.

Boning flyingfish, Barbados.

Trinidadian Cascadou   *Serves 4*

'Those who dine on cascadou will end their days in Trinidad.'

8 cascadous (crayfish will do)	4 tablespoons oil to fry
1 lemon or lime	2 onions, chopped
12g (¼oz) ginger	2 cloves garlic
salt and pepper to taste	4 tomatoes, chopped
cayenne pepper (optional)	1 litre (1¾pt) water

Clean the fish well, rub with lime or lemon juice and leave to stand for 15 minutes. Drain and season with ginger, salt, pepper and cayenne and allow to marinate. Place the fish in a frying pan with oil, and fry with onions, garlic and tomatoes. Add the water and bring to the boil, then simmer on a low heat for 30 minutes.

Serve with sweet potatoes, green bananas and cho-chos. You never know, you might end your days in Trinidad!

Crayfish Pelau

2 large crayfish
1 onion, chopped
2–3 cloves garlic, chopped
25 ml (1 fl oz) oil
1 teaspoon cumin
2 tomatoes, chopped

pepper and salt to taste
750 ml (1¼ pt) coconut milk
  (coconut cream mixed with
  water will do)
250 g (9 oz) long grain rice
1 bayleaf

Put the crayfish in boiling water until their shells turn pink (about 10–15 minutes). Drain and pour cold water over them. Crack the shells and remove the flesh and shred. Fry the onions and garlic for a few minutes then add the crayfish and cumin. Cook for 5 minutes. Stir in the tomatoes, salt, pepper and coconut milk, and simmer.

Wash the rice and add to the pan with a bayleaf. Bring to the boil and lower heat. Simmer for 25 minutes. Turn onto a serving dish and garnish with slices of hard-boiled egg and avocado.

This fish pelau recipe is suitable for crab, shrimps and white fish.

Good Friday Salmon

500 g (18 oz) salt salmon or
  1 450 g (1 lb) tin of pink salmon
juice of ½ lemon
2 tablespoons vinegar

1 onion, chopped
2 tablespoons olive oil
1 tomato, chopped
black pepper

Soak the salt salmon overnight with the juice of ½ a lemon. Discard the water and boil the fish in fresh water for 10–15 minutes with 2 tablespoons vinegar, then strain and flake. Do not boil tinned salmon, just flake. Fry onions and tomatoes in olive oil until golden, then add the flaked salmon and black pepper. Serve with Salamagundy Sauce (see page 63).

In Trinidad salted salmon is especially served on Good Fridays with vegetables and cucumber salad. Everything is cooked in olive oil and vinegar for religious reasons. Olive oil because it is pure and vinegar because it was the drink given to Christ on the cross.

Accra or Stamp and Go

250 g (9 oz) salt fish (prepared)
1 clove garlic
1 onion, chopped
sprig of thyme
chopped chives

black pepper
500 g (18 oz) self-raising flour
oil to deep fry
350 ml (12 fl oz) warm water

Shred the salt fish, add the garlic, onion, thyme and pepper and mix together well. Sieve the flour into a bowl and add the fish. Then gradually pour in the water to make a soft sticky batter. Beat well and drop spoonfuls of the mixture into hot oil, fry until golden. Serve hot for breakfast or as a snack.

Meat & Poultry

It was the Spanish who were responsible for introducing livestock to the Caribbean. They brought with them cattle, goats, chickens and pigs and once on the islands these animals bred quickly and soon were plentiful. Meat is now an important part of Caribbean cuisine, but it is interesting to note that the early slaves were not encouraged to eat it, although there was plenty available. Instead they were given salt fish and salt beef. It wasn't really until the abolition of slavery that meat was absorbed into traditional cooking. There were alternatives to beef, goat, chicken, mutton and pork: agouti, manicou, iguana, tortue and frogs were, and still are, a popular alternative source of protein and if you visit the islands you must try Mountain Chicken which is the name given to an edible frog called a crapaud. Crapaud is a delicacy in Dominica and Montserrat. Agouti, a small tailless mammal, is served as a speciality on many islands and the meat is quite gamey. There is a wonderful traditional story called 'Why the Agouti Has No Tail' in which the Agouti betrays his friend Dog and gets his tail bitten off as a result. It is said in the Caribbean that if you see a dog scratching at a hole in the ground he is looking for an agouti. In fact, dogs are used to hunt agouti and manicou in Trinidad. Manicou are small mammals and are normally smoked before cooking in stews or pelau. The flesh has a gamey flavour. Iguana is a large lizard that is a great favourite with many West Indians. Tatou are armadillos and are best eaten when just reaching maturity. They are cooked in their scales and taste similar to beef.

These traditional meats go back to the Arawak and Carib Indians and are still eaten in some country regions. I did find someone who took great delight in telling me how to catch and prepare them, but I have not included any recipes as I don't think these meats could be obtained in markets and there are no suitable substitutes for them. Goat meat is obtainable and curried goat is a popular and famous dish that's well worth a try.

Meat and poultry are usually seasoned and left to marinate for as long as possible and it is this seasoning and the method used to cook them that gives our meat dishes their uniquely Caribbean flavour. I personally find that beef does not need much seasoning or marinating as it tends to spoil the true flavour of the meat. I just use onion, tomato, garlic, salt and pepper and sometimes a little soy sauce. Chicken, poultry and pork do, however, benefit from seasoning and marination. Here is a list of all the seasonings I use for meat and poultry:

chilli (fresh or powdered)
onion
paprika
garlic cloves
garlic powder
nutmeg
coriander
cumin
thyme
chives
parsley
ginger
tomatoes
salt
black pepper
MSG
soy sauce
allspice

Barbecued Spare Ribs

2kg (4½lb) pork ribs	4 tablespoons honey
juice of ½ lemon	1 clove garlic, crushed
4 tablespoons soy sauce	½ teaspoon ginger
2 tablespoons vinegar	6 tablespoons beef stock
2 tablespoons sherry	

Wash the ribs with lemon. Mix all the ingredients together well and brush the marinade over the spare ribs. Leave to marinate for 2–3 hours. Remove the ribs from the marinade and put in a baking dish. Cook for 1 hour in a medium oven, 325°F (170°C, gas mark 3). It's wise to pour off excess fat and baste with the marinade during cooking. Serve hot with the marinade as a sauce. Alternatively, cook over a barbecue basting with the marinade.

Calypso Chicken   *Serves 4*

4 chicken breasts   2 green peppers, finely chopped
salt and pepper to taste   1 onion
chilli pepper (optional)   dash of Angostura bitters
1 clove garlic, crushed   ½ teaspoon saffron
pinch of cumin   2 tablespoons dark rum
pinch of MSG   300 ml (11 fl oz) chicken stock
1 slice of lemon and lemon juice 25 g (1 oz) coconut cream
4 tablespoons oil to fry

Wash and season the chicken with salt, pepper, garlic, cumin, MSG and lemon juice. Leave for 1 hour.

Fry the onion and green peppers until brown, add chicken and fry until golden. Put in the bitters, saffron, rum, stock and coconut cream, stirring well. Simmer on a low heat for 30 minutes. Serve with rice.

Fried Chicken

2 kg (4½ lb) chicken pieces   salt and pepper
1 onion, chopped   1 clove garlic, chopped
2 tomatoes, chopped   1 chilli pepper
1 sprig thyme   500 ml (18 fl oz) water
juice of 1 lemon   50 ml (2 fl oz) oil to fry

Clean and season the chicken with all the ingredients and leave to marinate. Take the chicken out of the marinade and fry in oil until brown. Allow the oil in the frying pan to cool, then add marinade and water and boil for 2 minutes then add the chicken. Cover and simmer for about 50 minutes or until the chicken is tender. Take off cover, turn up heat and cook for a further 10 minutes. Don't allow the water to dry out or the chicken to stick to the pan. The sauce should thicken by itself. Serve with rice or vegetables.

Chicken in Coconut and Pineapple

1.8kg (4lb) chicken, boned and cubed	2 coconuts
salt and pepper to taste	4 tablespoons oil
pinch of MSG	1 onion, chopped
1 clove garlic, chopped	dash of Tabasco sauce
pinch of cinnamon	1 small pineapple, sliced
4 teaspoons cornflour	3 tablespoons rum

Season the chicken with salt, pepper, MSG, garlic and cinnamon and leave to marinate.

Make 2 holes in the top of the coconuts, drain water and keep. Saw the shells in half and remove the flesh. Plug holes with foil and warm the shells in an oven preheated to 400°F (200°C, gas mark 6) for 5 minutes.

Fry the chicken for 5 minutes, add onion and Tabasco sauce and pour them into a saucepan. Liquidize the pineapple and coconut flesh and add to the saucepan. Mix the cornflour with the coconut water and stir into the chicken. Heat gently to boiling point, lower heat and simmer for 3 minutes. Remove from the heat and add the rum.

Pour the mixture into coconut shells and cover each one tightly with foil. Bake for 20–25 minutes in a medium oven, 350°F (190°C, gas mark 4). Serve with sliced yam, plantains and sweet potatoes or rice.

Brown Down Chicken

2 kg (4½ lb) chicken
1 onion, chopped
1 tomato, chopped
clove of garlic, chopped
chives, chopped
¼ teaspoon coriander
¼ teaspoon cumin
¼ teaspoon MSG

pinch of nutmeg
1 chilli pepper
salt and pepper
2 tablespoons oil
500 g (18 oz) potatoes
1 tablespoon sugar
knob of butter or margarine
150 ml (5 fl oz) water

Cut the chicken into pieces, clean and wash. Season with all the ingredients except the potatoes and sugar. Leave to marinate in the fridge (I always leave overnight).

Peel the potatoes and cut into small pieces. Heat the oil and sugar in a large, heavy saucepan until it turns dark brown and begins to burn. Shake off excess liquid from the chicken pieces, put in the saucepan with the potato and stir well so that all the pieces are covered with the browned sugar. Cover the pan and cook for 30 minutes in its own juice, stirring occasionally. Then pour in the marinade, water and butter. Stir well and simmer for 10 minutes. Serve with rice or vegetables.

Chicken Pelau

To cook Chicken Pelau follow the previous recipe but instead of the potatoes add:

500 g (18 oz) long grain rice
1.5 litres (2½ pt) water

After the chicken has cooked for 30 minutes pour in the washed rice and salted water. Bring to the boil and then simmer for 25 minutes or until the water has evaporated. Serve with tomato and cucumber salad.

Brown Down Beef

500 g (18 oz) frying steak
2 tablespoons oil
1 tablespoon sugar
250 g (9 oz) potatoes, diced
1 onion, chopped
pinch of thyme
150 ml (5 fl oz) water

pinch of MSG
salt and pepper to taste
2 tomatoes, chopped
pinch of parsley
25 g (1 oz) coconut cream
1 tablespoon soy sauce

Cut the meat into pieces, place in a bowl and season; onion and tomatoes are included in the seasoning as beef tastes better if it's not marinated. Heat the oil and sugar in a heavy saucepan until brown and starting to burn. Take the beef from the bowl and keep the seasoning. Put the beef and potatoes in the saucepan with the burnt sugar, stirring well. Lower the heat, cover and leave to cook for 30–40 minutes stirring occasionally. Add the seasoning, coconut cream and water and simmer for 10 minutes. Serve with plantains, eddoes, roast breadfruit or rice.

Cook Up

150g (5oz) salt meat (pork or beef)	sprig of thyme
2 tablespoons oil	dash of Tabasco sauce
2 teaspoons sugar	150ml (5floz) water
salt and pepper to taste	25g (1oz) coconut cream
1 onion, chopped	500g (18oz) rice
2 tomatoes, chopped	250g (9oz) cooked chicken or beef

Wash and cut up the salt meat and leave to soak overnight. Heat the oil and sugar in a large pan until it turns brown and begins to burn. Add the seasoning, which includes the onion and tomatoes, and fry for 3 minutes. Stir in salt meat and add water, coconut cream and rice. Bring to the boil, lower heat and simmer for 25 minutes stirring occasionally. Add the cooked meat and simmer for a further 15 minutes. Serve with avocado salad.

Sancoche

This is an old traditional plantation meal from Trinidad and is an easy-to-prepare, quick meal.

350g (12oz) salt beef or pork	2 green bananas
2 tablespoons oil	150g (5oz) yam
1 onion, chopped	4 okras
500ml (18floz) water	thyme
100g (4oz) lentils, washed	salt and pepper to taste
150g (5oz) tannias	

Wash, cut up and soak the salt meat overnight. Fry the onion in oil till golden brown, add salt meat and cook for 5 minutes. Add the water and bring to boil. Add lentils and cook for 20 minutes or until tender. Peel and slice tannia, green bananas, yams and okras, add them to the saucepan along with the thyme, salt and pepper. Cook for 20 minutes and serve.

Goat Water

This is a famous dish from Montserrat where it is served on special occasions. It's also served at 'house maroons' (house warming parties) to drive away evil spirits!

1.5 kg (3 lb) goat meat (lamb will do)
25 g (1 oz) butter
1 clove garlic, chopped
2 onions, chopped
salt and pepper
2 cloves
1 tablespoon tomato purée
2 litres (3½ pt) water
12 g (¼ oz) plain flour
50 g (2 oz) coconut cream
1 teaspoon Tabasco sauce

Wash the meat and cut up into pieces. Place in a large saucepan with all the ingredients except the flour, coconut cream and Tabasco sauce. Cover with water and bring to the boil then simmer on a very low heat for 2 hours. Blend the flour with a little water and then stir in. Next add the coconut cream and a dash of Tabasco sauce and cook until it thickens. Serve with rice and eddoes.

Curried Goat

In Jamaica this dish is usually eaten at parties or on festive occasions.

1 kg (2¼ lb) goat meat (lamb will do)
salt and pepper to taste
½ teaspoon allspice
3 tablespoons curry powder
1 clove garlic, chopped
pinch of cayenne pepper
750 ml (1¼ pt) water
2 potatoes, chopped
1 bayleaf
50 g (2 oz) coconut cream
dash of Tabasco sauce
2 tomatoes, chopped
2 onions, chopped
2 tablespoons oil

Wash and cut up the goat meat. Season with salt, pepper, allspice, curry powder, garlic, cayenne, onion and tomatoes, and leave to marinate for 1 hour.

Put the oil in a large saucepan and heat. Remove the meat from the seasoning and fry until brown. Add the water, potatoes and bayleaf and bring to the boil, lower heat and simmer for 1½–2 hours depending on how tender the meat is. Add the marinade, coconut cream and Tabasco, stir well and simmer for a further 10 minutes. Serve this famous Jamaican dish with rice or roti (see page 104).

Rum–Butter Steaks

4 tablespoons dark rum
1 onion, finely chopped
salt and pepper to taste
1 clove garlic, chopped

2 teaspoons lime or lemon juice
1 tablespoon chopped parsley
75 g (3 oz) butter
4 sirloin steaks

Put the rum in a saucepan over a low heat and add the onion, pepper, salt and garlic. Bring to the boil then lower the heat and allow to simmer for 3 minutes. Cool slightly then blend in the lime juice, parsley and butter then put in the fridge to chill. Season steaks with salt, pepper and garlic and grill or fry. Serve with a portion of rum butter on top of each steak.

Lamb Curry

1 kg (2¼ lb) lamb or mutton
1 tablespoon curry powder
1 teaspoon cumin
1 teaspoon coriander
salt and pepper to taste
1 chilli pepper, sliced
2 onions, sliced

2 tablespoons oil
500 g (18 oz) potatoes, sliced
1 green pepper, sliced
350 ml (12 fl oz) water
1 freshly grated coconut
1 tomato, sliced

Wash and season the lamb with curry powder, cumin, coriander, salt, pepper and chilli pepper. Fry the onions in oil until golden brown then add the potatoes, meat and green peppers. Add water and stir well, then simmer for 30–45 minutes or until the meat is tender. Stir in the grated coconut and tomatoes and simmer for a further 10 minutes. Serve with rice or vegetables. Curried beef is cooked in the same way.

Guyanese Pepper-pot

Pepper-pot originates from the Arawak Indians and can be kept going, with unseasoned meat being added to it, for days, weeks, months and, in the case of the Arawaks, even generations. No starchy food should be added, though, or it will turn sour. The pot is never washed but heated up every day to prevent the food going bad, similar to the French *pot-au-feu*.

The Guyanese claim that no true Pepper-pot is made without cassareep, a black syrup made from grated cassava root which is said to be a preservative and tenderizer. It is difficult to get hold of, so if you have none use gravy browning seasoned with black pepper.

1 oxtail or boiling chicken
1 kg (2¼ lb) lean pork belly
2.5 litres (4 pt) water
4 red peppers
sprig of thyme

150 ml (5 fl oz) cassareep or gravy browning seasoned with black pepper
2 onions
2 tablespoons brown sugar

Clean and cut the meat into pieces and put into a large saucepan with the water. Simmer for 2 hours. Add the peppers, thyme, onion, sugar and gravy or cassareep. Simmer for a further 45 minutes or until meat is tender. Serve as a main meal.

Souse

This is one of my favourite dishes, and is served at parties or festive occasions. No party is complete for me without this dish.

4 pig's trotters
water
juice of 2 lemons or limes
1 chopped onion

1 chilli pepper, chopped
watercress
½ cucumber, sliced
salt to taste

Wash and clean the trotters. Place in a pan and cover with water. Boil for 1½ hours or until tender. Remove from the heat, leave to cool and pour off the water. Put 600 ml (20 fl oz) of water in a casserole dish and add the lemon juice, onions, cucumber, chilli peppers, watercress and salt. Add the pig's trotters and leave to marinate overnight. Serve cold.

Jerked Pork Leg

Jerking is the original Arawak method of cooking a whole pig. The recipe was kept secret for many years and was passed down from generation to generation. Now it is widely known and is a popular dish all over the Caribbean. As a whole pig is a bit impractical I have used a leg of pork; you can even try the recipe with pork chops, it still tastes delicious.

2 kg (4½ lb) leg of pork
lemon juice
2 onions
25 g (1 oz) allspice
6–8 spring onions, chopped finely

2 bayleaves
2 chilli peppers
salt and pepper to taste

Wash pork with water and lemon juice. Blend all the seasonings together and spread all over the pork with your hands. Leave overnight to marinate.

Prepare a barbecue and when it's very hot place the leg of pork on a spit and cook over the charcoal, turning all the time. Throw some pimento berries or aromatic herbs onto the charcoal while the pork is cooking. This will give a nice flavour to the pork. It should take about 1½–2 hours to cook through but you must keep the barbecue hot all the time. Serve with roast breadfruit or salad.

Fried Crapaud

8 frogs' legs
salt and pepper to taste
50 g (2 oz) breadcrumbs

oil to deep fry
1 egg, beaten
lemon wedges

Trim the frogs' legs, wash and season with salt and pepper. Cover in breadcrumbs, dip in egg and dip in breadcrumbs again. Deep fry until golden. Serve as a starter with lemon wedges.

Braised Mountain Chicken

Both this recipe and Fried Crapaud have a strong French influence, as does a lot of the food in Dominica and Montserrat.

8 frogs' legs
salt and pepper to taste
1 clove garlic, chopped
2 tablespoons oil
1 carrot, thinly sliced

150 g (5 oz) mushrooms
150 ml (5 fl oz) white wine
150 ml (5 fl oz) water
1 tablespoon cornflour

Trim and wash the frogs' legs. Season with the salt, pepper and garlic and fry until golden. Place in a casserole dish with the carrots and mushrooms. Cover with the wine and water. Smooth the cornflour into a little water and stir into the casserole. Cook in a medium oven, 375°F (190°C, gas mark 4), for 35 minutes. Serve with rice.

Beef Patties

Patties used to be eaten at lunch but are now such a favourite they are eaten at any time. They are best eaten hot.

500 g (18 oz) minced beef
1 onion, finely chopped
1 chilli pepper
2 spring onions, finely chopped
50 ml (2 fl oz) oil
1 tablespoon curry powder

½ teaspoon cumin
pinch of dried thyme
salt and pepper to taste
250 g (9 oz) breadcrumbs
150 ml (5 fl oz) water

Pastry

300 g (11 oz) plain flour
½ tablespoon curry powder
pinch of salt

150 g (5 oz) margarine
cold water

Season the minced beef with the onions, pepper and spring onions and mix together well. Fry the mince in hot oil, stirring all the time. Add the curry powder, cumin, breadcrumbs, thyme, salt and pepper, mixing well. Stir in water and leave to simmer for 30 minutes. It's important that the mince is cooked moist, not too dry or too runny. Allow to cool.

To make the pastry

Sieve the flour, curry powder and salt into a bowl and mix in the margarine. Add enough water to hold the dough together. Leave in the fridge overnight.

Cut off a piece of the dough and roll out on a floured board to about 10 cm (4 inches) across. Cover half the circle with the filling and fold over, sealing the edges securely. Repeat until the dough and filling are used up. Place the patties on a baking tray and bake in a preheated oven at 400°F (200°C, gas mark 6) for 30 minutes.

Caribbean Christmas Turkey

In the Caribbean at Christmas turkey is served with callaloo, pigeon peas and rice. Sorrel is drunk with the meal or good old-fashioned rum. We celebrate Christmas to its fullest!

1 6kg (13lb) turkey	1 teaspoon chilli powder
3 onions, chopped	2 teaspoons ginger, grated
1 tablespoon chopped parsley	250 ml (9 fl oz) sherry
salt and pepper	2 lemons
2 cloves garlic, crushed	4 tablespoons rum
1 lemon	3 tablespoons vinegar
½ teaspoon MSG	2 tablespoons soy sauce
sprig of fresh thyme	4 rashers bacon

Clean and wash the turkey with lemon. Rub the salt and vinegar inside and out and leave in a cool place for a few hours. Wash the turkey and giblets well and season with all the ingredients except the bacon and leave to marinate overnight in the fridge.

I use two kinds of stuffing for the turkey, a breadfruit stuffing for the neck and a giblet stuffing for the body.

Breadfruit Stuffing

250 g (9 oz) cooked breadfruit or potatoes	salt and pepper
	1 tablespoon rum
100 g (4 oz) margarine	150 g (5 oz) cream crackers, crushed
50 ml (2 fl oz) evaporated milk	

Mash the cooked breadfruit or potatoes, add milk seasoning, rum and half the butter, mix well. Melt the remaining butter and mix in the crushed crackers. Blend the two mixtures together and stuff into the neck end of the turkey.

Giblet Stuffing

chopped giblets, seasoned (see method for Caribbean Christmas Turkey)	salt and pepper to taste
	1 onion, chopped
	6 rashers of bacon, chopped
350 g (12 oz) breadcrumbs	1 tablespoon oil
sprig of thyme	25 g (1 oz) butter
1 tablespoon chopped parsley	2 tablespoons sherry
chilli pepper	

Fry onions and bacon until brown and add chopped, seasoned giblets, parsley, thyme, chilli pepper, salt, pepper, breadcrumbs, sherry and butter. Mix together well, add a little water if too dry and stuff inside the body of the turkey.

Place the stuffed turkey on a baking dish and put 4 bacon rashers over the breast. Cover with foil and cook on a low heat, 300°F (150°C, gas mark 2), for 4–6 hours★ basting occasionally with marinade. When cooked, pour off juices into a saucepan and mix with a little cornflour to make the gravy; add a little water if necessary.

★N.B. Can be microwaved on medium, in a roasting bag, for 1½ hours (approximately 7 minutes per lb).

Vegetarian Dishes

The Rastafarians in the Caribbean are mainly vegetarian. They never touch swine flesh, shellfish, scaleless fish, snails or frogs. No salt or processed foods are used. All food is very carefully grown and cleanliness is of the highest order. Women who are menstruating are not allowed to prepare food for men. It is said that Rastafarian food is pure and 'I-tal'.

There are a lot of vegetarians who do not follow such a strict regime as the Rastafarians, so I have included a few special recipes with these people in mind.

All these dishes can, of course, be enjoyed by those who aren't vegetarian as well.

Melongene Baked in Coconut

2 large melongenes (aubergines)
1 chilli pepper, chopped
sprig of fresh thyme
4 onions, chopped
600 ml (1¼ pt) coconut milk
salt (if required)

Peel the melongenes and cut into thin slices. Place in a shallow dish. Put onions, pepper and thyme on top and pour on coconut milk. Cover and put in a medium oven, 350°F (176°C, gas mark 3), for 50 minutes, taking off the cover for the last 10 minutes. Serve hot.

Sweet Potato and Banana Casserole

500 g (18 oz) sweet potatoes
150 g (5 oz) butter
3 large bananas, sliced
juice of 2 oranges

Cook the potatoes in their skins and allow to cool. Peel and cut into slices. Line a casserole dish with a layer of slices and spread butter on top. Arrange a layer of banana slices over this and butter. Repeat, ending with a layer of bananas and butter. Pour on orange juice and bake in a medium oven, 360°F (180°C, gas mark 4), for 30 minutes. Serve hot.

sweet potato

Sweet Potato Coconut

2 sweet potatoes, baked	50 g (2 oz) butter or margarine
3 tablespoons stout	salt and pepper to taste
50 g (2 oz) freshly grated coconut	50 g (2 oz) grated cheese

Halve the sweet potatoes and carefully remove the flesh, making sure the skins are not broken. Mash the potato with butter and add the coconut and stout. Blend together well and replace mixture into the skins. Sprinkle some cheese on each one and put under the grill to brown. Serve with salad.

Banana Curry

2 onions, chopped	25 g (1 oz) curry powder
1 apple, chopped	350 ml (12 fl oz) milk and water
50 g (2 oz) sultanas, washed	(50/50)
50 g (2 oz) cashew nuts, crushed	25 g (1 oz) coconut cream
50 g (2 oz) butter or margarine	4 bananas, chopped
25 g (1 oz) plain flour	

Fry the onions until golden then add the apple, sultanas and nuts. Mix the flour and curry into a paste with a little water, add to the pan and cook for 3 minutes stirring continuously. Pour in the milk and water and coconut cream. Stir until the mixture thickens. Add the bananas and cook gently for 5 minutes. Serve with rice.

Roast Corn

When I was a child in Trinidad we used to have roast corn as a meal during harvest time. We would pick the cobs from the field and cook them straightaway. We used to play a game to see who could get the most grains of corn from one cob. They were so sweet and I have never tasted corn like them anywhere else. Perhaps it was because they were so fresh.

4 fresh cobs of corn butter or
  margarine

Strip the corn and put under grill or barbecue until golden brown. Serve with butter.

Scalloped Tomatoes and Okra

25 g (1 oz) cornflour
25 g (1 oz) butter or margarine,
  melted
250 ml (9 fl oz) milk
salt and pepper to taste
½ tablespoon chopped parsley

4 tomatoes, sliced
8 okras, cooked
4 tablespoons breadcrumbs,
  seasoned with nutmeg and
  black pepper

Sieve the cornflour and blend with melted butter, stirring continuously for 2 minutes. Take off the heat and gently pour in the milk. Return to the heat, add salt, pepper and parsley and simmer for 5 minutes.

Put the tomatoes and sliced okra in an ovenproof dish and cover with most of the breadcrumbs, then pour the sauce over the top. Sprinkle the remaining breadcrumbs on top and bake in a medium oven, 350°F (176°C, gas mark 3), for 20 minutes. Serve with yams, spinach, cho-chos or rice.

Rice Pelau

500 g (18 oz) rice
2 onions, chopped
2 tomatoes, chopped
sprig of fresh thyme
25 g (1 oz) butter

chopped chives
1 litre (1¾ pt) water
50 g (2 oz) coconut cream
salt and pepper to taste

Wash and soak the rice for 1 hour then drain. Fry the onions, tomatoes and thyme then add rice, stirring well until golden. Add the water, coconut cream, pepper and salt. Bring to the boil then lower the heat and simmer for 15 minutes. Serve with an avocado salad.

Akkra Cakes

This is very similar to an Egyptian dish called Falafel.

250 g (9 oz) black eye peas,   salt and pepper to taste
  cooked   1 tablespoon milk
1 green pepper   fat for frying

Skin the black eye peas and put in a blender with green pepper and seasoning. Drop spoonfuls of the mixture into hot fat and fry until golden. Serve hot.

Chana

Children love chana and I remember spending my pocket money on it after school in Trinidad.

500 g (18 oz) chick peas   oil to deep fry
salt and pepper to taste

Soak the chick peas overnight. Drain and dry in a cloth. Heat the oil and deep-fry the peas until golden. Place on a couple of layers of kitchen tissue to absorb the excess oil and season with salt and pepper.
  Serve as an appetizer or at parties instead of peanuts.

Eddoe Soufflé

500 g (18 oz) eddoes   2 eggs, separated
juice of ½ lemon   salt and pepper to taste
25 g (1 oz) butter or margarine   25 g (1 oz) grated cheese
150 ml (5 fl oz) milk

Peel and wash the eddoes. Place in boiling water with the lemon juice and cook for 25 minutes. Drain water and mash well, add butter, milk, seasoning and egg yolk. Mix together well. Whisk egg whites to a stiff consistency and blend into the mixture. Put into a soufflé dish, sprinkle cheese on top and cook in a hot oven, 400°F (200°C, gas mark 6), for 20 minutes. Serve immediately.
  This soufflé can also be made from yam, sweet potatoes, breadfruit, cassava or pumpkin.

Pumpkin Pancakes

250 g (9 oz) cooked pumpkin pinch of allspice
25 g (1 oz) sugar   oil to fry
1 egg
50 g (2 oz) self-raising flour

Liquidize pumpkin with other ingredients. Heat the oil in a frying pan until smoking. Pour a spoonful of the mixture into the pan. Fry until golden and serve with honey.

Desserts, Puddings & Ice Creams

The people of the Caribbean definitely have a sweet tooth and this is borne out by the dozens of sweet recipes I've been told; enough to fill a whole book, in fact! Of course, we do have so many delicious fruits and sweet things to use as ingredients: bananas, mangoes, guava, coconuts, etc.

It was hard deciding which of the recipes to include in this chapter, I hope there are a few here that take your fancy.

Ice Cream

Once when I was five years old I was put in charge of the ice-cream-making tub at my brother's christening. That meant I had to turn the handle of the tub that was used to make home-made ice cream. I was the envy of my other brothers and sisters.

The tub was wooden and had a stainless-steel drum in the centre where the ice-cream mixture was put. Chipped ice and salt was then put between the wood and the drum. The drum had a handle attached to it and the idea was to keep churning the drum until eventually the mixture froze. Then the delicious ice cream was served. My mum used to make all sorts of ice-cream in this way: soursop, banana, coconut and mango, and they were all out of this world. Nowadays ice cream tastes just as good made in a freezer but for me it just hasn't got the same magic as making it in that old ice-cream tub. Here are some of my favourite ice-cream recipes.

Guava Ice Cream

12 ripe or tinned guavas	150 g (5 oz) sugar
1.2 litres (2 pt) water	2 eggs, beaten
250 ml (9 fl oz) milk	juice of 1 lime or lemon
1 400 g (14 oz) tin of evaporated milk	1 teaspoon vanilla flavouring

Wash and chop the guavas and boil them for 1 hour in the water. When cool rub them through a sieve. Mix the tinned and fresh milks with the sugar and bring them slowly up to almost boiling point. Stir in the beaten eggs until the mixture thickens but do not

allow the mixture to boil. Remove from the heat and stir in the guava, lime juice and vanilla flavouring and beat together well. Pour into a freezer tray and freeze for 1 hour then take out and put in a blender and blend until smooth. Repeat this process of freezing and blending twice and this will make the ice-cream soft and smooth.

Mango Ice Cream

1 400g (14oz) tin of evaporated milk
600ml (1¼pt) milk
1 egg, beaten

150g (5oz) sugar
250g (9oz) mango pulp
1 teaspoon lime or lemon juice
2 drops vanilla flavouring

Heat the tinned and fresh milks then stir in the sugar and beaten egg stirring all the time until the mixture thickens; do not allow the mixture to boil. Leave to cool then add the mango, lime juice and flavouring. Put into a blender and blend well. Pour into a freezer tray and freeze for 1 hour. Blend and freeze again twice then leave to set.

Banana and Almond Ice Cream

1 400g (14oz) tin of evaporated milk
250ml (9floz) milk
150g (5oz) sugar
2 eggs, beaten

3 mashed bananas
juice of 1 lemon or lime
1 teaspoon vanilla flavouring
50g (2oz) chopped roasted almonds

Heat the tinned and fresh milks and stir in the sugar until it has dissolved. Beat in the eggs until the mixture thickens; do not allow it to boil. Allow to cool then add the mashed bananas, juice and flavouring. Put into a blender and blend well. Pour into a freezer tray and freeze for 1 hour, then blend again and return to the freezer. Serve with a sprinkling of crushed roasted almonds.

Rum Ice Cream

600 ml (1¼ pt) milk
4 eggs, beaten
50 g (2 oz) castor sugar
4 tablespoons rum (cherry
  brandy, or ginger wine)

250 ml (9 fl oz) single cream
½ teaspoon vanilla flavouring

Warm the milk and stir in the eggs and sugar. Stir until the mixture thickens, then leave to cool. Blend in the rum, cream and flavouring and pour into a container and freeze for 45 minutes. Blend again and return to freezer. Serve with orange rind or grated pineapple.

Coconut and Pineapple Ice Cream

750 ml (1¼ pt) water
1 coconut, grated
2 eggs, beaten
1 400 g (14 oz) tin of condensed
  milk

2 drops vanilla flavouring
juice of 1 lime or lemon
1 pineapple, grated

Add the water to the grated coconut and extract the milk by straining it through a fine muslin cloth or sieve. Heat coconut milk and stir in eggs, condensed milk, flavouring and lemon juice.

Stir constantly, do not allow to boil, leave to cool then add pineapple. Pour into a container and freeze until set then blend and freeze again. Serve with flaked chocolate.

Soursop Ice Cream

1 large soursop
500 ml (18 fl oz) boiling water
1 400 g (14 oz) tin of condensed
  milk

1 400 g (14 oz) tin of evaporated
  milk
½ teaspoon vanilla flavouring

SOURSOP

Wash and peel the soursop and remove the inner core. Mash and add to boiling water. Leave to cool then strain through a sieve, making sure to extract all the juice. Add the condensed milk to the juice then stir in the evaporated milk and flavouring. Pour into a container and freeze. If you can't find a fresh soursop then use a 500 ml (18 fl oz) tin of soursop juice, but don't use the boiling water.

Avocado Ice Cream

600 ml (1¼ pt) milk
2 eggs, beaten
250 g (9 oz) castor sugar

2 avocados, mashed
½ teaspoon vanilla flavouring

Heat the milk then add eggs and sugar, stirring constantly until the mixture thickens. Leave to cool. Blend the avocados and flavouring into the mixture. Pour into a container and freeze until set, then blend and freeze again. Serve with almond wafers.

Pineapple Sherbet

1 finely pineapple, chopped
juice of 1 orange

600 ml (1¼ pt) milk
250 g (9 oz) castor sugar

Mix the pineapple and orange juice together. Heat the milk and stir in sugar. Leave to cool in the fridge until chilled. Mix the pineapple and milk together and stir well. Freeze until set, then blend and re-freeze. Decorate with pieces of pineapple and serve.

Shave Ice

Children love shave ice and as kids we used to buy it during break at school. It was sold by ladies who carried big trays laden with sugar cake, pone, guava cheese and chana and to buy any one of these was considered 5 cents well spent.

4 trays ice cubes
150 ml (5 fl oz) orange, lemon or
  pineapple juice
paper cups

Crush the ice as finely as possible and pack into the paper cups. Pour on the juice and serve.

Mango Sorbet

600 ml (1¼ pt) water
250 g (9 oz) sugar
600 ml (1¼ pt) mango purée

Boil the water and sugar together for 10 minutes than leave to cool. Stir in the mango purée, pour into a container and freeze for 1 hour then blend again. Repeat twice to get a smooth texture. Serve with slices of fresh mango on top.

Pawpaw Sorbet

500 ml (18 fl oz) water
250 g (9 oz) sugar
1 pawpaw puréed

Boil the water and sugar together for 10 minutes. Leave to cool then add the purée and blend well. Pour into a container and freeze for 1 hour. Take out and blend again and return to the freezer. Repeat twice. Serve with almond biscuits.

pawpaw

Coconut Cream Jelly

1 freshly grated coconut
 (save the coconut water)
150 ml (5 fl oz) milk

1 tablespoon gelatine
1 200 g (7 oz) tin of condensed
 milk

Pour the milk and coconut water over the grated coconut and leave for 45 minutes. Strain through a sieve to extract all the juice and discard the pulp. Stir gelatine into the mixture and leave to dissolve for 10 minutes. Heat the mixture stirring constantly, do not boil. Stir in the condensed milk then pour the mixture into a mould and leave to set.

Coffee Jelly

500 g (18 oz) marshmallows
500 ml (18 fl oz) hot black coffee

1 egg white, beaten
150 ml (5 fl oz) whipped cream

Melt the marshmallows in hot coffee over a low heat. Pour into a dish and when nearly set whisk in the beaten egg white. Spoon into small dishes and leave to set. Cover with whipped cream and serve.

Ginger Wine Jelly

25 g (1 oz) gelatine
500 ml (18 fl oz) water
250 g (9 oz) castor sugar

50 ml (2 fl oz) ginger wine
juice of 1 orange
juice of 1 lime or lemon

Leave the gelatine to soak in a little water for 5 minutes. Boil rest of the water and pour in the gelatine and sugar, stirring constantly for 10 minutes. Mix in the ginger wine and juices, pour into a wet mould and leave to set.

Ginger Fool

50 g (2 oz) preserved ginger,
  chopped
2 tablespoons rum

250 ml (9 fl oz) whipped cream
50 g (2 oz) castor sugar

Mix all the ingredients together in a blender. Spoon into individual glasses and chill. Serve with pieces of finely chopped ginger on top.

Mango Fool

purée of 4 ripe mangoes
50 g (2 oz) castor sugar
250 ml (9 fl oz) double cream

Add the sugar and cream to the mango purée and whip together well. Spoon into individual glasses and chill. Serve with brandy snaps or almond biscuits.

Rum Fool

50 g (2 oz) castor sugar
250 ml (9 fl oz) double or
  whipped cream

4 tablespoons rum
juice of 1 lime

Blend all the ingredients together well and spoon into glasses. Chill and decorate with flaked chocolate.

Exotic Fruit Salad

4 bananas
½ pawpaw, chopped
2 mangoes, chopped
2 tablespoons rum (optional)

2 oranges or tangerines in
  segments
½ pineapple, chopped
4 ripe guavas, chopped

Mix all the fruit together with rum, leave to chill and serve with whipped cream.

Rum and Banana Flambé

50 ml (2 fl oz) milk
150 g (5 oz) brown sugar
25 g (1 oz) melted butter

6 bananas
250 ml (9 fl oz) rum
50 g (2 oz) chopped nuts

Heat the milk, add the sugar and butter. Bring to the boil stirring constantly. Peel bananas, slice lengthways and arrange in an ovenproof dish. Cook in a medium oven, 375°F (190°C, gas mark 5), for 10 minutes. Pour on the mixture, half the rum and sprinkle with chopped nuts and return to the oven for a further 10 minutes. Pour the rest of the rum over the dish just before serving and set alight at the table. It always makes an exciting sight.

Banana Pudding

4 slices of bread, buttered and
  diced
150 g (5 oz) chopped nuts
4 bananas, sliced
50 g (2 oz) brown sugar

2 teaspoons grated orange rind
2 eggs, beaten
500 ml (18 fl oz) milk
pinch of allspice

Spread half the bread in a greased pie dish and sprinkle half the nuts on top. Arrange the sliced bananas on top and sprinkle with sugar and orange rind. Put the rest of the nuts and bread on top. Mix eggs and milk together and pour over the bread. Sprinkle allspice on top and bake in a medium oven, 375°F (190°C, gas mark 5), for 40 minutes.

Orange Supreme

3 oranges	2 egg whites
250 ml (9 fl oz) milk	pinch of salt
3 eggs, beaten	2 drops vanilla flavouring
250 g (9 oz) castor sugar	

Peel and slice the oranges and arrange in a dish. Heat the milk and add the flavouring, the eggs and half the sugar, stirring continuously until the mixture thickens. Pour it over the oranges. Cool in the fridge for 2–3 hours. Whisk the egg whites and gradually blend in the rest of the sugar and the salt, whisk until stiff. Cover the chilled oranges with the egg mixture and place under a pre-heated grill for 30 seconds. Serve at once.

Sea Moss Jelly

25 g (1 oz) dry sea moss	1 tablespoon rum
150 ml (5 fl oz) water	pinch of allspice
150 ml (5 fl oz) milk	drop of vanilla flavouring
50 g (2 oz) sugar	
3 drops food colouring (cochineal)	

Soak the sea moss in a little water for 3 hours then simmer until tender. Drain and put into the fresh water and simmer for about 1 hour. Strain then add the milk, sugar, rum, flavouring, allspice and food colouring, stirring well. Pour into a mould and leave to set. This jelly has a unique taste and it can be made into a drink by swizzling a tablespoon of the jelly into a glass of milk and adding a dash of Angostura bitters and a sprinkling of nutmeg.

Marisule
St. Lucia

Sweet Potato Pone

1 kg (2¼ lb) sweet potato, peeled and grated
50 g (2 oz) raisins
50 g (2 oz) melted butter
½ teaspoon grated ginger
250 g (9 oz) pumpkin
1 teaspoon vanilla flavouring

250 g (9 oz) sugar
50 g (2 oz) sultanas
1 teaspoon allspice
1 grated coconut or 250 g (9 oz) desiccated coconut
250 ml (9 fl oz) water

Mix all the ingredients together and pour into a greased oven dish and bake for 1 hour in a medium oven, 375°F (190°C, gas mark 5).★ Serve hot or cold.

★N.B. Can be microwaved on high for 6–7 minutes or until; cooked when tested in the centre.

Cassava Pone

This pudding is a Christmas speciality in Barbados.

250 g (9 oz) grated sweet cassava
250 g (9 oz) pumpkin
1 teaspoon allspice
600 ml (1¼ pt) milk

1 grated coconut or 250 g (9 oz) desiccated coconut
1 teaspoon vanilla flavouring
250 g (9 oz) sugar

Mix all ingredients together and pour into a greased oven dish and bake for 1 hour at 375°F (190°C, gas mark 5).★ Serve hot with ice-cream or cold on its own.

*N.B. Can be microwaved on high for 6–7 minutes or until cooked when tested in the centre.

Cornmeal Pone

250 g (9 oz) cornmeal
25 g (1 oz) butter
50 g (2 oz) sugar
½ teaspoon allspice

600 ml (1¼ pt) milk
4 tablespoons molasses
75 g (3 oz) sultanas

Heat the milk and gradually stir in the cornmeal. Blend in all the other ingredients and pour into a greased oven dish and bake for 2 hours at 375°F (190°C, gas mark 5).* Serve hot or cold.

*N.B. Can be microwaved on high for 5–6 minutes or until cooked when tested in the centre.

Mango Flan

1 tablespoon gelatine
150 ml (5 fl oz) water
½ teaspoon vanilla flavouring

100 g (4 oz) sugar
6–8 mangoes, sliced
25 cm (10 in) flan case

Soak the gelatine in a little water. Add the rest of the water, flavouring and sugar, stirring constantly until the mixture thickens. Leave to cool then arrange the mango slices in the flan case and cover them with the syrup. Chill and serve with cream.

Coconut Tart

make up coconut water to
   100 ml (4 fl oz) with ordinary
   water
75–100 g (3–4 oz) sugar
½ teaspoon vanilla flavouring
1 pinch allspice

1 coconut, grated
150 g (5 oz) shortcrust pastry
150 ml (5 fl oz) whipping cream
1 tablespoon jam (strawberry
   will do)

Heat the water and add sugar, flavouring and spice, then add the grated coconut. Simmer until the mixture thickens. Line a flan tin with pastry and spread with jam, pour the coconut mixture over the top and bake in a medium oven, 375°F (190°C, gas mark 5), for 25 minutes. Leave to cool. Whisk the cream and spread on the tart, chill and serve.

Guava Pie

1 dozen guavas, peeled and
  chopped, or 1 400g (14oz) tin
  will do
500ml (18fl oz) water

250g (9oz) castor sugar
2 drops almond essence
250g (9oz) shortcrust pastry

Put the guavas in a saucepan with the water, essence and sugar
and simmer for 15 minutes. Take out the guavas and quickly boil
the liquid until it thickens. Use half the pastry to line a pie dish
and pour in the guavas and syrup. Cover with pastry and seal
round edges. Pierce top with a fork and bake in a medium oven,
375°F (190°C, gas mark 5), for 45 minutes.

If using tinned guavas, there is no need to cook them, just put
them straight into the pastry with the syrup. Serve hot or cold
with ice-cream.

Daddy's Dukanoo

My father told me his mother used to cook this for him when he
was a child. Sometimes they had it as a savoury with meat added
to the ingredients. Cornmeal can be used in place of the sweet
potatoes. This recipe was probably
brought to the West Indies by
the African slaves as there are
several parts of Africa where
it is still cooked today. This
is one recipe that has been
well and truly passed on.

500g (18oz) sweet potatoes,
  grated
250g (9oz) sugar
pinch of salt
½ teaspoon grated nutmeg

150g (5oz) flour
50g (2oz) butter
plantain or banana leaves or foil
  cut into 15cm (6in) squares

Mix all the ingredients into a dough, adding a little water if
necessary. Put a spoonful of the mixture on each leaf, tie up with
string and cook in boiling water for 1 hour.

Breads (Sweet & Savoury), Buns, Cakes & Cookies

At one time flour in the Caribbean was made from the sweet cassava by the Arawak Indians and even today the method still survives. The bread it made could be kept for many months without going stale. Although bread is still made from cassava flour in the traditional way, wheat flour is now more commonly used.

Fruit and vegetables play an important part in the baking of bread and cakes. Coconut and bananas, sweet potato and corn are all used to produce a wide variety of interesting cakes and breads.

Bakes are a quick and easy alternative to conventional bread and are eaten for breakfast or supper. Rotis are another special favourite and can be served with curry at parties or instead of rice at mealtimes. Cakes and buns are baked and eaten with great enthusiasm and are always a welcome snack.

Bakes

250 g (9 oz) self-raising flour
pinch of salt
25 g (1 oz) margarine

50–75 ml (2–3 fl oz) water
oil to fry

Sift the flour, add salt and rub in the margarine. Gradually add the water and knead the mixture into a soft dough. Cut the dough into small balls, flatten them and fry in hot oil until golden brown. Serve hot or cold for breakfast.

I love bakes best with salt fish but they can be served with cheese, jam, honey or butter. You can also make bakes in the oven. Don't cut into balls, just knead it flat in a greased baking tin and bake for 25–30 minutes in a medium oven, 375°F (190°C, gas mark 5).

Corn Bread

150 g (5 oz) cornmeal
2 teaspoons baking powder
500 ml (18 fl oz) milk
1 tablespoon brown sugar
150 g (5 oz) flour

1 egg, beaten
150 g (5 oz) butter or margarine,
   melted
pinch of salt

Place cornmeal in a bowl, then sift in baking powder and salt. Add sugar, eggs, milk and cooled melted butter and mix well. Pour mixture into a baking tin and bake in a hot oven, 400°F (200°C, gas mark 6), for 25 minutes.★

★N.B. Can be microwaved on high for 5–6 minutes.

Roti

Roti can be eaten as a main meal and are always a big hit at parties filled with delicious curry. I love roti and can eat them till the cows come home; my record to date is nine rotis one after the other!

Making Roti, and cleaning Rice, Trinidad

Roti was introduced to the Caribbean by the Asians. They sometimes have theirs filled with Dal Puri (a split pea mixture).

The last time I visited Trinidad, I was lounging on the beautiful Maracas Bay beach and an Asian family were having a roti lunch. It smelt delicious. They must have seen my mouth watering because they came over with one for me and, boy, was it good!

You see, once you're hooked on rotis you're really hooked. Try them and see what I mean.

500g (18oz) white or wholemeal flour
½ teaspoon bicarbonate of soda
½ teaspoon salt

50g (2oz) butter
milk or water to mix
oil

Sift the flour, bicarbonate and salt into bowl. Mix into a stiff dough with a little milk. Cut into small balls then roll them flat. Spread a little oil on each and roll back into a ball and leave for a while. Roll out again and cook on a hot greased baking stone or griddle, turning repeatedly, for about 5–7 minutes. Wrap curry in the middle and eat with your fingers.

Orange Bread

50g (2oz) brown sugar
150g (5oz) butter or margarine
rind of 1 orange
3 eggs, separated

250g (9oz) self-raising flour, sifted
4 tablespoons orange juice
pinch of salt

Blend the sugar and butter together into a creamy mixture and add the orange rind and egg yolks. Gradually add the sifted flour, salt and orange juice. Whisk the egg whites stiffly and blend into the mixture. Pour the mixture into a baking tin and cook in a medium oven, 375°F (190°C, gas mark 5), for 1 hour.★

★N.B. Can be microwaved on high for 6–8 minutes.

Banana Bread

175g (6oz) brown sugar
150g (5oz) butter or margarine
1 egg, beaten
4 ripe bananas, mashed
250g (9oz) self-raising flour

pinch of nutmeg
pinch of salt
4 drops vanilla flavouring
150ml (5floz) milk

Cream the sugar and butter together until smooth. Add the egg and bananas and beat well. Gradually mix in the flour, nutmeg, salt, vanilla and milk. Mix well. Put the mixture in a baking tin and bake for 1 hour in a medium oven, 375°F (190°C, gas mark 5).★

★N.B. Can be microwaved on high for 6–8 minutes.

Sweet Bread

My mother used to make sweet bread every weekend when we were kids and no Sunday morning was complete without a slice.

Sweet-bread is always baked at Easter or Christmas time or when you have special guests. It can be eaten at teatime or for a snack. I love a slice grilled with peanut butter on top.

500g (18oz) self-raising flour
150g (5oz) brown sugar
pinch of salt
1 egg, beaten
50g (2oz) melted margarine
rind of an orange
50g (5oz) coconut, freshly
  grated or desiccated

½ teaspoon vanilla flavouring
200ml (7floz) milk and water
  (50/50)
½ teaspoon allspice
150g (5oz) mixed fruit

Sift the flour and salt into a bowl and mix in all the other ingredients. Adding a little water and milk at a time, knead into a sticky dough taking care not to let it become too runny. Cut in two, roll out on a floured board and shape. Put into non-stick baking tins and bake in a medium oven, 375°F (190°C, gas mark 5), for 1 hour. ★Take out of the oven, melt a teaspoon of sugar in a little water and glaze the loaves while still hot.

★N.B. Can be microwaved on low for 12 minutes.

Coconut Drops

250 g (9 oz) self-raising flour
175 g (6 oz) brown sugar
pinch of allspice
75 ml (3 fl oz) milk
rind of ½ orange

150 g (5 oz) coconut, freshly
  grated or desiccated
3 drops vanilla flavouring
25 g (1 oz) margarine
pinch of salt

Sift the flour into a bowl and add all the ingredients, adding the milk a little at a time. Mix well. Drop spoonfuls of the mixture onto a non-stick baking sheet and bake in a hot oven, 425°F (220°C, gas mark 7), for 15–20 minutes. Serve as a snack. Children love these. Try them with a glass of lemonade.

Chocolate Buns

75 g (3 oz) butter
175 g (6 oz) sugar
250 g (9 oz) self-raising flour
2 tablespoons cocoa powder

pinch of salt
1 egg, beaten
3 tablespoons milk
½ teaspoon vanilla flavouring

In a bowl, cream the butter and sugar together, sift the flour, cocoa and salt into the bowl and mix well. Gradually add egg, flavouring and milk. Knead lightly and cut into small pieces. Place them on a non-stick baking sheet and bake in a hot oven, 425°F (220°C, gas mark 7), for 15–20 minutes.

Jamaican Buns

50 g (2 oz) dried yeast
250 g (9 oz) butter or margarine,
  melted
150 ml (5 fl oz) brown sugar
1 egg, beaten
500 g (18 oz) flour

pinch of salt
250 g (9 oz) mixed fruit
2 teaspoons allspice
½ teaspoon vanilla flavouring
2 tablespoons molasses
150 ml (5 fl oz) milk

Dissolve the yeast in a little warm water and leave until the mixture is frothy (about 30 minutes). Blend the butter, sugar and egg together. Sieve the flour and salt together in a bowl with the yeast mixture. Add the butter mixture and the fruit, allspice, flavouring and molasses, and gradually pour in the milk. Knead into a soft dough and leave to rise in a warm place for about 2 hours until double its size. Knead again on a floured board then cut into small buns and place on a non-stick baking tray and bake in a medium oven, 375°F (190°C, gas mark 5), for 30 minutes. Glaze with a little sugar and water while still hot.

Nut Bun

250g (9oz) self-raising flour
pinch of salt
150g (5oz) chopped nuts
50ml (2floz) milk
150g (5oz) brown sugar
1 egg, beaten
150g (5oz) chopped dates

Sift the flour and salt into a bowl and add the sugar. Mix in the egg, milk, nuts and dates, stirring well. Pour into a round non-stick baking tin and bake in a medium oven, 375°F (190°C, gas mark 5), for 1 hour.

Peanut Specials

2 egg whites
2 drops vanilla flavouring
3 teaspoons cornflour
150g (5oz) peanuts, shelled and chopped
50g (2oz) castor sugar

Whisk egg whites until very stiff, add sugar gradually with cornflour, nuts and flavouring. Drop spoonfuls onto a non-stick baking tray and bake in a hot oven, 425°F (220°C, gas mark 7), for 10 minutes.

Sweet Potato Cookies

250g (9oz) sweet potato, mashed
25g (1oz) sugar
pinch of salt
pinch of cinnamon
50g (2oz) melted butter
250g (9oz) self-raising flour
50ml (2floz) milk

Blend together the potato, butter and milk. Sift in the flour and add all the other ingredients. Knead lightly and roll out to about 6mm (¼inch) thick. Cut the cookies out with a shape cutter or the rim of a glass. Place them on a non-stick baking tray and bake in a hot oven, 425°F (220°C, gas mark 7), for 15 minutes. Makes 12–15 cookies.

Banana Cookies

1 egg yolk
75g (3oz) castor sugar
50g (2oz) butter or margarine
250g (9oz) self-raising flour
2 ripe bananas, mashed
pinch of salt
½ teaspoon vanilla flavouring

Blend the egg, sugar and butter together. Mix in the flour and salt and stir to a creamy mixture. Blend in the bananas and flavouring. Knead lightly and roll out to about $\frac{1}{4}$ inch thick. Cut out with a shape cutter and place on a non-stick baking tray. Bake in a hot oven, 425°F (220°C, gas mark 7), for 15 minutes. Makes 12–15 cookies.

Orange and Nutmeg Cookies

100g (4oz) castor sugar
2 eggs, beaten
rind of 3 oranges
3 drops almond essence

$\frac{3}{4}$ teaspoon nutmeg
150g (5oz) self-raising flour
25g (1oz) chopped walnuts

nutmeg and mace.

Gradually mix the sugar and eggs into a creamy smooth mixture. Blend in flour, nutmeg, nuts, rind and essence.

Spread the mixture onto a non-stick baking tray and bake in a medium hot oven, 375°F (190°C, gas mark 5), for 30 minutes. Cut into slices and remove when cool.

Rum Cake

250g (9oz) butter
375g (13oz) castor sugar
6 eggs
juice and rind of 4 limes

50g (2oz) cornmeal
250g (9oz) self-raising flour
50ml (2floz) dark rum
150g (5oz) dark chocolate

Cream the butter and gradually add the sugar. Add the eggs one at a time with lime juice and rind, beat well. Sift in the cornmeal and flour blending well, stir in rum. Put the mixture into a non-stick cake tin and bake for 1 hour in a medium oven, 375°F (190°C, gas mark 5).★ Pour on 2 tablespoons rum while still hot. Melt the chocolate and spread on top and leave to cool.

★N.B. Can be microwaved on high for 6–8 minutes or until cooked when tested in the centre.

Steel Drum Cake

A cake with a difference for children's birthday parties.

3 eggs, separated	150 g (5 oz) self-raising flour
150 g (5 oz) castor sugar	rind of 1 lemon
25 g (1 oz) cocoa	

Icing

250 g (9 oz) icing sugar	1 egg
½ teaspoon lemon rind	2 tablespoons water

Whisk the egg white until stiff and gradually stir in half the sugar. Mix the egg yolk and rind and add the rest of the sugar. Mix the egg white and yolk together and stir in the cocoa and flour, pour into a shallow cake tin and bake in a moderate oven, 350°F (180°C, gas mark 4), for 30 minutes.★ Mix the icing and when the cake is cool, ice it with a steel drum design.

★N.B. Can be microwaved on high for 4–5 minutes or until cooked when tested, in the centre.

West Indian Christmas Cake

Christmas is a time of great excitement in the Caribbean. The celebrations and traditions go back to the time of the slaves, who looked forward to Christmas because for three days, Christmas Day, Boxing Day and New Year's Day, they were allowed their only holiday of the year.

At Christmas time there has always been celebrations and dances, some of which have African origins. Christmas time in Jamaica and the Bahamas is 'Junkanoo' season when groups of people parade through the streets dancing to exciting African rhythms and wearing symbolic costumes.

One of the best traditions is the making of Christmas cake. West Indian Christmas cake is totally unique. Its origins are English but we have adapted the recipe and, of course, added vast quantities of rum. We start 'soaking the fruits' (raisins, sultanas and currants in rum) weeks or even months before Christmas and by the time it's ready to bake it is well and truly saturated with flavour.

I like to make my cake according to my mum's recipe, which makes an incredible wet and gooey cake, just how I like it! Her recipe has been passed on to her children, who in turn will pass it on to her eleven grandchildren, and so it will go on. Now I am passing it on to you with the compliments of my mum.

550 g (18 oz) sultanas
500 g (18 oz) raisins
500 g (18 oz) currants
1 bottle of dark rum
500 g (18 oz) butter or margarine
500 g (18 oz) brown sugar
12 eggs
rind of 1 lemon
700 g (2 lb) plain flour
pinch of salt

1 teaspoon allspice
250 g (9 oz) molasses
150 g (5 oz) glacé cherries, chopped
½ teaspoon vanilla flavouring
1 tablespoon gravy browning (as colouring)
50 g (2 oz) ground almonds
250 g (9 oz) chopped mixed nuts
½ bottle of brandy

Wash the dried fruits and soak them in rum in an airtight container for about 1 month (it will still be sensational if you haven't got a whole month). Cream the butter and sugar together. Gradually add the eggs and lemon rind. Sift the flour, salt and spices into the mixture then add molasses, cherries, flavouring, gravy browning, ground almonds and nuts. Now add the soaked fruits and rum, mixing well.

Line two 18-cm (7-inch) cake tins with greaseproof paper (this stops the cake from burning and keeps it moist). Pour in the mixture and bake in a low oven, 300°F (150°C, gas mark 2), for 3–4 hours.* Test the cake by piercing with a knife. If the blade comes out clean then the cake is cooked. Pour the brandy over the cakes while they are hot and leave to cool overnight before removing them from the tin.

Store the cakes in airtight tins and after a week they can be covered in almond paste or marzipan, iced with royal icing and decorated. Merry Christmas!

*N.B. Can be microwaved on low for 30–40 minutes (for each cake) or until cooked when tested in the centre.

Sweets & Confections

A few favourites I used to love as a child and still do!

Tuloons

250 ml (9 fl oz) molasses
50 g (2 oz) sugar
½ teaspoon grated ginger

1 pinch allspice
1 grated coconut or 175 g (6 oz)
  desiccated coconut

Boil the molasses, sugar and spices into a syrup. Remove from heat and stir in coconut, mix well. Drop spoonfuls onto a baking tray and leave to set.

Tamarind Balls

250 g (9 oz) tamarind pulp
500 g (18 oz) sugar

Mix the two ingredients together well and roll into balls. Coat with sugar and store in an airtight container.

Guava Cheese

12 ripe guavas or 1 400g (14oz) tin of guavas
250g (9oz) sugar

Wash, peel and rub the guavas through a sieve (pour away the syrup if using tinned guavas). Add the sugar and boil stirring constantly until the mixture shrinks from the sides of the pan. Pour onto a baking sheet and leave to set. Cut into pieces and dust with castor sugar.

Pineapple Fudge

1 grated pineapple
500g (18oz) sugar

Boil the sugar and pineapple together into a syrup, stirring constantly. Pour onto a non-stick baking sheet and leave to set. Cut into squares.

Sugar Cake

350g (12oz) sugar
3 drops food colouring
175ml (6floz) water

250g (9oz) grated coconut
2 drops vanilla flavouring

Boil the sugar and water together, drop a little into cold water and it should form a soft ball. Remove syrup from heat and stir in coconut and flavouring. Pour half the mixture into a greased tin. Colour the remainder and pour over the first layer. Cut into shapes when cool.

Ginger Snaps

2 tablespoons grated ginger
25 ml (1 fl oz) water
250 g (9 oz) sugar

25 g (1 oz) butter
1 teaspoon lime juice

Put the water, sugar and ginger into a pan and boil until the mixture forms into a ball. Remove from the heat and add lime juice and butter stirring rapidly. Pour onto a greased baking tray and just before it sets cut into squares.

Lime Toffee

juice of 2 limes
250 g (9 oz) sugar

50 g (2 oz) melted butter or
   margarine

Stir together lime juice, sugar and butter. Boil for 15 minutes stirring gently all the time. Pour onto a greased baking tray, leave till half set then cut into pieces and leave to harden.

Drinks, Non-Alcoholic & Alcoholic

Rum is always associated with the Caribbean, and rightly so since it's our national drink. Rum is distilled from molasses and aged in oak casks which gives it a golden colour, the darker rums being coloured with caramel. Many types of rum are produced in the Caribbean and exported all over the world, from the light white Bacardi to the heavy dark Trinidadian rum. We consume rum all year round but never more so than at Christmas or Carnival time.

Some folk also believe that white rum sprinkled around a new house or building will ward off 'jumbies' or evil spirits. Rum is also used for medicinal purposes as a liniment or poured on the top of the head as a cure for colds and fevers. It, of course, makes an ideal base for cocktails and punches and coupled with the exotic fruits of the islands makes for an endless variety of cool refreshing drinks. The Caribbean is indeed a cocktail drinker's paradise!

It's worth mentioning three other important cocktail ingredients that are produced in the Caribbean. The first is Curaçao, which is a delightful orange liqueur produced on the island of the same name, the second is Tia Maria, a coffee liqueur produced in Jamaica, and the third is Angostura bitters, which is produced exclusively in Trinidad to a secret recipe invented by a Dr Siegert.

I personally don't drink alcohol but that doesn't stop me from mixing these drinks for my friends. I also love thinking up exciting non-alcoholic cocktails and punches for myself and the children.

Non-alcoholic Drinks
Pineapple Drink

Save your fresh pineapple skins and make this delicious drink. Add melon skins as well if you have any.

skin of 1 pineapple
1.25 litres (2 pt) water
dash of Angostura bitters

2 cloves
sugar to taste

Boil the water and pour over the skins and cloves. Leave for a while then strain, sweeten and serve with crushed ice and a dash of bitters.

Banana Swizzle

3 ripe bananas
750 ml (1¼ pt) milk
4 drops almond essence

3 tablespoons clear honey
3 drops vanilla flavouring
nutmeg to garnish

Liquidize all the ingredients together and leave to chill. Serve in tall glasses with a sprinkling of nutmeg on top.

Banana Nectar

6 bananas
juice of 2 oranges
sugar if needed

juice of 2 limes
250 ml (9 fl oz) water

Liquidize all the ingredients together, chill and serve with crushed ice.

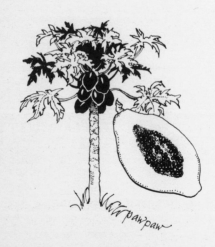

pawpaw

Mango and Pawpaw Cocktail

Some say that this cocktail is high in digestive enzymes and is an antidote for over eating. It's usually served at Christmas.

150 ml (5 fl oz) mango juice
150 ml (5 fl oz) pawpaw juice
100 ml (3 fl oz) fresh lime juice

2 tablespoons honey
cherries to decorate

Liquidize all the juices together with honey and chill. Decorate with a cherry and serve.

Benji Cocktail

1 litre (1¾ pt) cream soda
juice of 2 limes
dash of Angostura bitters

plenty of crushed ice
cherries and chunks of pineapple
 to decorate

Liquidize the cream soda, lime juice and ice together for 15 seconds. Pour into glasses, add a dash of bitters and decorate with cherries and pineapple.

Mixed Citrus Cordial

juice of 4 oranges
juice of 2 limes or lemons
juice of 2 grapefruits

juice of 4 tangerines
6 tablespoons water
6 tablespoons sugar

Boil the water and sugar together to make a syrup and leave to cool. Mix the juices together and chill, then pour in the syrup and top up with crushed ice. Decorate with slices of orange or lemon.

Mawby Cordial

The Arawak Indians were the first people to boil the bark of the mawby tree to make this refreshing bitter-sweet drink.

50 g (2 oz) mawby bark
4 cloves
piece of dried orange peel

piece of cinnamon stick
500 ml (18 fl oz) water

Boil all the ingredients together for 5 minutes. Cool and leave in the fridge in an airtight jar. This mawby cordial has to be diluted before it can be served, as follows:

Mawby Drink

2 tablespoons mawby cordial
1 litre (1¾ pt) water
sugar to taste (it takes a lot of
 sugar!)

1 drop aniseed oil

Mix all the ingredients together and leave overnight. Whisk till frothy and serve with ice. This drink is quite bitter but very refreshing.

Fruit Punch

1 litre (1¾ pt) orange juice
juice of 4 limes
1 litre (1¾ pt) pineapple juice
2 litres (3½ pt) soda water, iced
  water or lemonade
1 teaspoon nutmeg

dash of Angostura bitters
1 banana, chopped
pineapple chunks
sugar if necessary
sprig of fresh mint

Mix all the ingredients together in a punch bowl and serve chilled with ice.

Mammy's Ginger Beer

In Trinidad we make this drink at Christmas time and no Christmas goes by without my mum making it.

3 litres (5 pt) water
150 g (5 oz) grated ginger
piece of orange peel
1 kg (2½ lb) sugar

Angostura bitters
cloves
1 tablespoon lemon juice

Boil the water and pour onto the ginger, lemon juice and orange peel and leave overnight. Strain then sweeten and add dash of bitters. Seal into bottles with a clove in each and leave in a warm place for 3–4 days. Then serve with ice.

Guava Drink

8–10 ripe guavas
1 litre (1¾ pt) water

sugar to taste
1 pinch nutmeg

Blend all the ingredients together then strain and serve with crushed ice.

Soursop Punch

1 soursop
piece of lime peel
1 litre (1¾ pt) water
1 400 g (14 oz) tin of evaporated
  milk

dash of Angostura bitters
1/2 teaspoon vanilla flavouring
sugar to taste

SOURSOP

Wash and peel the soursop. Liquidize or mash with lime peel. Add 600 ml (1¼ pt) of the water, mix well and strain into a jug. Repeat with the rest of the water, making sure all the juice is extracted, then discard the pulp. Stir in the milk, sugar, bitters and flavouring and leave to chill. To serve, coat the rim of the glasses with icing sugar and fill with soursop juice and ice.

Carrot Juice

250 g (9 oz) grated carrots
1 litre (1¾ pt) water
1 400 g (14 oz) tin of condensed
  milk
1 170 g (6 oz) tin of evaporated
  milk

dash of Angostura bitters
2 drops almond essence
sugar if necessary

Mix together the water and grated carrots, leave for a while then squeeze through a strainer. Stir in the milk, bitters and essence and a little sugar if required. Chill and serve with ice.

Orange Nog

350 ml (12 fl oz) orange juice
1 egg, beaten
sugar to taste

grated orange peel
2 drops vanilla flavouring
dash of Angostura bitters

Blend all the ingredients and serve with plenty of crushed ice.
Decorate with a sprinkling of grated orange peel.

Pineapple and Ginger Punch

1 pineapple, cubed
12 maraschino cherries
2 tablespoons sugar
½ litre (1 pt) ginger beer

1 orange, sliced
¼ teaspoon ginger
juice of 1 lime
½ litre (1 pt) lemonade

Mix the fruit with the sugar and ginger and leave to stand for 2
hours. Add the ginger beer, lemonade and lime juice and serve
chilled with ice.

Alcoholic Cocktails and Punches

Bim Bam Boo

25 ml (1 fl oz) sweet vermouth
2 dashes orange Curaçao
100 ml (4 fl oz) dark rum

dash of bitters
crushed ice

Shake in a cocktail shaker. Serve in chilled glasses.

Banana Daiquiri

100 ml (4 fl oz) white rum
juice of 1 lime

1 banana, sliced
25 g (1 oz) sugar

Blend all the ingredients and serve with crushed ice.

Coconut Cream Daiquiri

50 ml (2 fl oz) white rum
juice of 1 lime
25 g (1 oz) coconut cream

Blend all the ingredients together. Serve with crushed ice.

Hibiscus

100 ml (4 fl oz) white rum
1 tablespoon Pimm's No. 1
2 tablespoons orange juice

2 tablespoons pineapple juice
2 tablespoons lime juice

Shake all the ingredients and serve with ice.

J.A.

100 ml (4 fl oz) white rum
75 ml (3 fl oz) water

juice of 1 lime
1 sprig fresh mint

Stir all the ingredients together. Serve with ice.

Spiced Cocktail

175 ml (6 fl oz) rum
75 ml (3 fl oz) sweet vermouth

pinch of cinnamon
juice of 1 orange

Mix the orange, rum, cinnamon and vermouth well. Strain and pour into chilled glasses with ice.

Zombie

juice of 2 oranges
juice of 1 grapefruit
100 ml (4 fl oz) golden rum
1 tablespoon soft brown sugar
crushed ice

juice of 2 lemons
100 ml (4 fl oz) white rum
100 ml (4 fl oz) dark rum
2 dashes Angostura bitters

Pour the fruit juices over the ice and add the sugar and rum. Stir well, add bitters, stir again. Serve in chilled glasses.

Bajan Punch

600 ml (1¼ pt) rum
600 ml (1¼ pt) pineapple juice
300 ml (12 fl oz) iced water
chunks of pineapple
slices of cucumber
ice
juice of 3 oranges

juice of 3 lemons
slices of lemon
slices of orange
3 dashes Angostura bitters

Put the ice in a punch bowl and pour the fruit juices, rum and bitters over it. Stir well and add water. Garnish with slices of fruit and cucumber. Leave to stand for a while then serve.

Orange Punch

slices of orange
2 dashes of Angostura bitters
2 tablespoons sugar
600 ml (1¼ pt) white rum

2 tablespoons Curaçao
juice of 6 oranges
1 syphon of soda water

Put plenty of ice in a punch bowl, pour on orange juice, rum, Curaçao, sugar and bitters. Mix together well and garnish with orange slices. Squirt in the soda just before serving.

Ginger Wine

5 litres (9 pt) water
50 g (2 oz) ginger
500 g (18 oz) raisins

1 kg (2½ lb) brown sugar
3 limes, sliced and peeled

Boil the water and add the ginger and raisins. Simmer for 30 minutes then stir in sugar and limes. Leave to cool, strain and pour into bottles. It is ready to drink in about 2 weeks.

Egg Nog

Good for convalescents.

2 tablespoons rum
2 eggs
honey to taste
600 ml (1¼ pt) milk

piece of lemon rind
2 drops vanilla flavouring
pinch of nutmeg

Beat the eggs, add milk, lemon rind, rum, flavouring and honey. Sprinkle nutmeg on top and serve.

Punch-à-Crema

Delicious at Christmas or on special occasions.

6 eggs
1 400 g (14 oz) tin of evaporated
  milk
1 400 g (14 oz) tin of condensed
  milk
½ bottle rum

½ teaspoon vanilla flavouring
2 teaspoons Angostura bitters
lemon rind
sugar to taste
cherries

L   eggs with lemon rind then add the milk, rum,
         bitters and sugar. Serve with crushed ice and garnish
         ies.

Carnival Punch

A drink to turn any gathering into a carnival!

Play Mas, Play Mas
It's Carnival time so come and Play Mas
Jump up, dance with the band
It's Carnival time so come and Play Mas.

600 ml (1¼ pt) dark rum
4 tablespoons Benedictine
2 tablespoons golden syrup
juice of 2 oranges
300 ml (11 fl oz) brandy

2 teaspoons Angostura bitters
juice of 4 grapefruits
pinch of nutmeg
ice
rind of lemon or lime

Mix the juices and syrup together well. Stir in the rum, brandy, bitters and Benedictine. Add the ice and stir in the nutmeg and lemon rind. Serve.

Planters' Punch

100 ml (4 fl oz) water
4 tablespoons castor sugar
100 ml (4 fl oz) dark rum

juice of 3 limes
1 orange, sliced
dash of Angostura bitters

Mix the sugar and water together and add rum, lime juice and bitters. Stir well, serve with crushed ice and decorate with orange slices.

Hangover Healer

2 teaspoons Worcestershire sauce
1 teaspoon vinegar

pinch of salt and pepper
1 egg

Mix the sauce and vinegar with salt and pepper. Add the egg, taking care not to break the yolk, and swallow without breaking the yolk.

A saviour for the morning after the night before.

Teas & Medicines

With the recent interest being shown in homeopathic medicine, and the publicity it has been receiving, it is interesting to note that the people of the Caribbean have been using natural homeopathic remedies for centuries. Most of them came with the slaves from Africa and were passed down from generation to generation. Many people swear by these traditional cures and use them in preference to modern pills and medicines. Folk remedies are complex and should only be practised by those who have studied the subject and know what they are doing. But here are a few simple ones that my mother swears by and I have found to be effective.

nutmeg and mace

Spiced Tea

Good for colds and flu.

3–4 mace blades
275 ml (½ pt) water
honey to taste

¼ teaspoon grated nutmeg
milk to taste

Boil the mace for 15 minutes. Strain and add the nutmeg and honey. Serve hot with a splash of milk if required.

Ginger Tea

Wonderful for stomach ache, nausea or travel sickness.

600 ml (1¼ pt) water
1 large piece ginger, chopped
honey to taste

Boil the ginger in the water for 10 minutes. Strain and add honey to taste.

Mint Tea

Helps to settle indigestion and colic.

4 mint leaves
500 ml (18 fl oz) water
honey to taste

Boil the mint leaves in water for 5 minutes then add honey to taste. Serve after a meal.

Orange Peel Tea

Helps to calm the nerves and heartburn and also settles the stomach.

peel of 1 orange
500 ml (18 fl oz) water
honey to taste

Boil the orange peel for 10 minutes, sweeten with honey.

Nutmeg Tea

Drink last thing at night for insomnia and headaches.

½ nutmeg, grated
250 ml (9 fl oz) water
honey to taste

Boil the water, add the nutmeg and sweeten with honey if required.

Watercress

Eat to help clear blood and skin disorders.

Sea Moss Jelly (see page 99)

Good for bronchial and kidney ailments as well as bowel disorders.

Okra

The okra plant can be used for healing external ulcers and sores.

Pawpaw Leaves

Pawpaw leaves as well as the juice are used to treat liver and stomach complaints and to overcome dyspepsia and gastric ailments. Pawpaw leaves can also be used as a meat tenderizer.

Plantain

Plantains make an excellent poultice which can be used to remove splinters and for relieving boils and bruises. For insect bites, crush the leaves, dip them in hot water and apply to affected area.

Sugar Cane

The juice and pith are used to relieve hoarseness and tickly coughs.

Garlic

Garlic is well known for its medicinal properties. It can be used to treat coughs and catarrh as well as digestive problems.

Specialities of the Islands

As I said in my introduction, the Caribbean islands differ enormously and although many of the fruits and vegetables are the same, each island has its own very special dishes. If you are contemplating a visit to the Caribbean it's worth knowing the specialities of each of the islands, and your Caribbean dinner guests will be very impressed if you can serve a dish that is special to their island.

Some of the dishes listed below are particular to an island because of the influence of the countries that colonized them. For instance, in the Spanish-influenced islands, Arroz con Pollo (rice and chicken) is a speciality. In other cases a dish is eaten because there is an abundance of a particular fish or animal on the island, for example, flying fish are very common in the sea around Barbados and, of course, the Bajans are experts at cooking it.

Antigua

Dukanoo (sweet potato pudding)
Pepper-pot soup
Salt fish
Fungi (savoury cornmeal pudding)
Stuffed crab back
Pumpkin soup
Lobster
Red snapper
Man soup (fish soup)

Aruba and Curaçao

Sopito (chowder)
Calas (bean fritters)
Keshi yena (stuffed cheese)
Ayacas (leaf-wrapped meat)
Pastechi (meat pasties)
Stoba (goat or lamb stew)
Boterkoek (butter biscuits)
Cachapas (cornmeal pancakes)

Barbados

Flying fish
Cassava pone (Christmas speciality)
Sea eggs (sea urchins)
Jug-jug (Guinea corn, peas and meat Christmas dish)
Pepper-pot stew
Conch fritters
Langouste (lobster)
Coo-coo
Souse (marinated pig's trotters)
Mawby
Sea moss jelly

Dominica

Crapaud (frogs' legs)
Lambi (fried conch)
Agouti
Manicou
Tannia soup
Sea moss drink

Dominican Republic

Chicharrones de pollo (fried chicken)
Chicharrones (crisp pork rind)
Yuca (fried cassava)
Moro de habicuelas (rice and peas)
Sancocho (meat stew)
Mofongo (plantain balls)

Grenada

Carrot soup
Callaloo (soup with spinach and crab)
Lambi souse (marinated conch)
Jack and bluggoe soup (fish and banana soup)
Soursop fool
Guava and nutmeg jellies

Guadeloupe

Blaff (fish in broth)
Court bouillon (fish in spicy sauce)
Boudin (black pudding)
Colombo (meat or fish curry)
Sea eggs
Land crab omelette

Haiti

Tassan de dinde (dried turkey)
Riz au djon djon (rice and black
  mushrooms)
Groits de porc (fried pork)
Sauce ti-malice (tart sauce)
Salt fish salad

Jamaica

Ackee and salt fish
Jerk pork (barbecued pork)
Curried goat
Pepperpot soup
Salamagundy (herring salad)
Escoveitch fish (marinated
  fish)
Stamp and Go (salt fish fritters)
Dukanoo
Matrimony (star apple and
  orange dessert)

Martinique

Sea urchins
Octopus
Conch
Soudins (clams)
Accra (salt fish fritters)
Court bouillon
Blaff

Montserrat

Goat water (goat stew)
Crapaud

Puerto Rico

Arroz con pollo
Jueyes (land crab in its shell)
Fried goat
Asopao (rice with meat and
  seafood stew)

Morcillas (spicy black
  pudding)
Pechon asado (roast suckling
  pig)

St Kitts and Nevis

Lambi
Crab back
Boija (coconut and cornmeal
  bread)
Goat water
Salt fish fried with melongene

St Lucia

Callaloo soup
Pumpkin soup
Crab back
Fried plantains
Stuffed breadfruit

St Vincent

Stewed shark
Callaloo
Arrowroot cake

Trinidad and Tobago

Pigeon peas and rice
Chip chip (small clams)
Callaloo
Roti
Curried shark
Sancoche (meat and vegetable
  stew)
Pelau (rice with meat or fish)
Souse
Cascadou
Tatou (armadillo)
Manicou
Agouti
Sorrel
Ginger beer

Mealtimes & Menus

West Indians love their food and all their meals are large. Breakfast is normally eaten between 5 and 8 a.m. and can consist of anything that takes ones fancy . . . fungi, green bananas, pap, sweet bread, salt fish or even bacon and eggs.

Lunch is eaten the same time as in England – 12–2 p.m. – and one big soup dish may be served or a main dish with several side dishes. Sometimes a starter may be served and, of course, there is always a sweet at the end of the meal.

Dinner can be served as early as 4 p.m. This is a custom from the days of slavery when the slaves had their dinner on their return from work on the plantations. They started work at dawn and finished about 3–4 p.m.

Dinner is once again a large meal very similar to lunch. The day might be ended with a snack such as cassava pone and cocoa.

Here are a few typical menus both for everyday meals and special occasions.

Breakfast
Cornmeal Pap
or Fresh Pawpaw

Salt Fish Buljou and Fried bakes
or Fungi and Salt Fish
with Green Bananas
Sweet Bread
or Orange Bread
Tea★

★All hot drinks are called tea, even coffee, cocoa and chocolate.

Lunch
Lobster Salad
or Avocado Soup

Crab Back
or Brown Down Beef
with Coconut Rice
Plantains
Yams
Sweet Potatoes

Mango Ice Cream or Cassava Pone

Dinner
Melongene Baked in Coconut
or Scalloped Tomatoes and Okra

Pepperpot Soup
or Chicken Pelau
or Pepper-pot Stew★
or Caribbean Baked Fish

Coo-coo, Rice or Green Bananas

Pineapple Sherbert
or Coconut Tart
or Frost and Flame Bananas

★Not eaten with a starter.

Sunday Lunch
This is a grand affair and only the best tablecloths and crockery
are used. It is the largest meal of the day and later dinner might
not be eaten. Poultry or meat is always served.

Brown Down Chicken
or Fried Chicken
or Jerked Pork

Vegetable Mayonnaise Salad
Rice and Peas
Fried Plantains
Sweet Potatoes, Yams
Cucumber Salad

Guava Ice Cream
or Dukanoo
or Rum and Banana Flambé
or Sweet Potato Pone

Soursop Punch
Mawby
Carrot Juice

Carnival Menu

Cook Up Pigeon Peas and Rice
Tomato Salad
Coconut and Pineapple Ice Cream
Sweet Bread
Steel Drum Cake

Carnival Punch
Pineapple Drink
Plenty of rum

Good Friday Lunch

Avocado Salad

Salt Salmon
Sweet Potato, Dasheen
Plantains
Cucumber Salad

Exotic Fruit Salad
or Mango Fool
or Sea Moss Jelly
or Coconut Drops

Limeade

Party Menu

Roti and Curry Goat
Beef Patties – Souse
Chana – Roast Corn – Salads
Sugar Cake

Zombie
Fruit Punch (non-alcoholic)
Bajan Punch

Christmas Dinner

Christmas Rum Punch

Roast Turkey with Stuffing
Roast Pork
Callaloo
Macaroni Pie
Sweet Potatoes
Yams
Eddoes
Fried Plantain
Green Bananas
Vegetable Mayonnaise Salad
Green Salad

Christmas Cake
Soursop Ice Cream
Pawpaw Sorbet

Sorrel
Ginger Beer
Punch-à-Crema
Mawby
Rum

INDEX